NAVIGATING THE DIGITAL NOMAD LIFESTYLE

THE POWER OF INTROSPECTION AND EMOTIONAL INTELLIGENCE

CONNECTNOMADS   contact@connectnomads.com

NAVIGATING THE DIGITAL NOMAD LIFESTYLE

"Discover the power of introspection and emotional intelligence for enhancing your digital nomad lifestyle. This book provides practical exercises, techniques, and strategies for self-discovery and self-awareness, including journaling prompts, mindfulness practices, and life planning workbook. Learn how to find clarity and direction in life, reduce distractions, and stay motivated on your personal growth journey. With a focus on the unique challenges and opportunities of the digital nomad lifestyle, this guide is essential for anyone seeking greater happiness, fulfillment, and success on the road."

CONNECT NOMADS DIGITAL ELIBRARY

What is ConnectNomads.com

ConnectNomads.com is a comprehensive platform designed for digital nomads and remote workers seeking resources, guidance, and community. Offering valuable information on topics such as remote work opportunities, travel planning, and lifestyle management, ConnectNomads.com aims to empower location-independent professionals to thrive in their careers while exploring the world.

How this book is structured?

This book is designed to serve as a comprehensive guide for digital nomads, offering insights and advice on various aspects of self-discovery and personal growth. It is not intended to be read in one go, but rather as a set of guidelines that provide valuable takeaways for different ideas and aspects of the nomadic lifestyle. As you explore the chapters, you may notice some overlap between topics, as certain strategies are commonly applicable across different areas of personal development. Feel free to read at your own pace, revisiting sections as needed, and drawing inspiration from the diverse range of concepts and techniques presented throughout the book.

If you have any ideas on new input, or even corrections, we are more than happy to hear from you, and if our editors like and accept the input then – if you are comfortable with it – we will include in our next update with credit noted for you.

Email us – contact@connectnomads.com

Mentions

We would like to clarify that throughout this book, we have not received any monetary gain or inducements for mentioning any connections, people, or resources. Our primary goal is to share valuable insights and tips that can genuinely help digital nomads in their journey of self-discovery and personal growth. The only exceptions to this are individuals or resources identified as ConnectNomads Members on our website. These members are part of our community and support our mission. We maintain transparency and prioritize the authenticity of the information shared, ensuring that our readers can trust the guidance provided in this book.

Our Digital Library

The ConnectNomads.com library offers members a diverse collection of free eBooks, providing invaluable insights and practical advice on a variety of topics related to the digital nomad lifestyle. From remote work strategies to travel tips and personal development, these eBooks are a valuable resource for location-independent professionals seeking to enhance their skills, knowledge, and overall experience.

Please visit http://www.connectnomad.com to see if there are any other publications which might interest you.

CONTENTS

INTRODUCTION

The Rise of Digital Nomadism

In recent years, the concept of location independence has gained significant traction, revolutionizing the way people live, work, and travel. Digital nomadism has emerged as a popular lifestyle choice for those who seek freedom, flexibility, and the opportunity to explore the world while maintaining a fulfilling career. Enabled by advances in technology and the growing acceptance of remote work, this movement continues to reshape traditional notions of work-life balance.

Digital nomadism is not just about working from a laptop on a beach or sipping coffee in a trendy co-working space; it's about embracing a mindset that values experiences and personal growth over material possessions and conventional definitions of success. It's about redefining what it means to live a meaningful life and seizing opportunities to learn, grow, and make a positive impact on the world.

As more people become aware of the potential benefits of a location-independent lifestyle, the demand for resources and guidance on how to successfully navigate this unconventional path has increased. "Digital Nomad Mastery: A Comprehensive Guide to Building a Successful Location-Independent Lifestyle" aims to provide aspiring and experienced digital nomads with the tools, knowledge, and inspiration they need to thrive in this exciting and ever-evolving landscape.

In this book, we will cover a wide range of topics crucial to achieving digital nomad mastery, from assessing your skills and finding remote work opportunities to managing finances, planning your travels, and adapting to new cultures. We will also discuss the importance of maintaining a healthy work-life balance, giving back to the communities you visit, and cultivating resilience and adaptability in the face of challenges.

By the end of this guide, you will have a solid understanding of the essential components of a successful location-independent lifestyle and be well-equipped to embark on your own journey toward digital nomad mastery. So, let's begin this adventure and explore the possibilities that await in the world of location independence.

CHAPTER 1: INTRODUCTION TO INTROSPECTION AND EMOTIONAL INTELLIGENCE FOR DIGITAL NOMADS

Definition of introspection and emotional intelligence and their significance for digital nomads

The unique challenges and opportunities of the digital nomad lifestyle and how self-discovery and self-awareness can enhance it

The digital nomad lifestyle, where individuals leverage technology to work remotely and travel the world, presents unique challenges and opportunities. Embracing self-discovery and self-awareness can significantly enhance this lifestyle, enabling digital nomads to make the most of their experiences.

Challenges:

- Maintaining work-life balance: Digital nomads may struggle with setting boundaries, as their work and personal life often blend together. Developing self-awareness can help them recognize when to step away from work and prioritize their well-being.

- Loneliness and social isolation: Constantly changing locations can make it difficult to form lasting connections. Fostering self-discovery can encourage digital nomads to explore new activities or groups, expanding their social circle.

- Adapting to new environments: Digital nomads must quickly adapt to unfamiliar places, cultures, and languages. Building self-awareness can help them identify their strengths and weaknesses, making it easier to acclimate to new surroundings.

Opportunities:

- Personal growth: The digital nomad lifestyle provides ample opportunity for self-discovery, as individuals encounter new people, cultures, and experiences. Embracing these opportunities can lead to personal growth, increased confidence, and a more authentic understanding of oneself.

- Expanding professional horizons: Remote work can expose digital nomads to diverse industries, clients, and projects. By embracing self-awareness, they can identify their passions and skills, paving the way for career advancement and satisfaction.

- Building a global network: Digital nomads can create a vast network of personal and professional connections across the globe. Developing self-awareness can enable them to better understand their communication and relationship-building styles, enhancing these connections.

To maximize the benefits of the digital nomad lifestyle, individuals should engage in regular self-reflection, journaling, and mindfulness practices. This can promote self-discovery and self-awareness, ultimately enhancing their overall experience as a digital nomad.

An overview of the connection between introspection, emotional intelligence, and personal fulfilment for digital nomads

Introspection, emotional intelligence, and personal fulfilment are interconnected concepts that can greatly impact the lives of digital nomads. By understanding and nurturing these connections, digital nomads can enhance their overall well-being and satisfaction with their chosen lifestyle.

- Introspection: Introspection refers to the process of self-examination and reflection on one's thoughts, emotions, and experiences. For digital nomads, introspection can help them gain a deeper understanding of their motivations, desires, and values. Regular introspection enables digital nomads to make informed decisions about their career paths, relationships, and the places they choose to live and work. Introspective practices such as journaling, meditation, or engaging in thought-provoking conversations can provide valuable insights.

- Emotional intelligence (EI): EI refers to the ability to recognize, understand, and manage one's emotions and those of others. It involves four key components: self-awareness, self-management, social awareness, and relationship management. Digital nomads can benefit from developing their EI in several ways. First, it can help them adapt to new environments by understanding their emotional reactions and adjusting accordingly. Second, EI can improve communication and relationship-building skills, which are essential for maintaining connections despite the nomadic lifestyle. Lastly, EI can help digital nomads cope with the challenges of remote work and maintain a healthy work-life balance.

- Personal fulfilment: Personal fulfilment is the sense of satisfaction and contentment that comes from living a life that aligns with one's values, passions, and goals. For digital nomads, introspection and EI can directly contribute to personal fulfilment. Introspection helps them identify their core values and goals, while EI enables them to navigate the complexities of their lives more effectively. As a result, digital nomads can make choices that lead to greater satisfaction and alignment with their true selves.

In summary, the connection between introspection, emotional intelligence, and personal fulfilment is vital for digital nomads. By engaging in regular introspective practices and cultivating their emotional intelligence, digital nomads can make informed decisions, build meaningful relationships, and live a life that truly reflects their values and aspirations. This, in turn, leads to greater personal fulfilment and satisfaction with their unique lifestyle.

Why introspection and emotional intelligence are crucial for digital nomads in navigating the complexities of remote work and travel.

Introspection and emotional intelligence (EI) are crucial for digital nomads as they navigate the complexities of remote work and travel. These skills help them adapt to new environments, manage stress, maintain relationships, and make informed decisions, ultimately leading to a more fulfilling and successful lifestyle. Here's why introspection and EI are essential for digital nomads:

- Adapting to new environments: Digital nomads frequently move to unfamiliar places with different cultures, languages, and customs. Introspection allows them to reflect on their experiences, feelings, and reactions to these changes. Meanwhile, EI enables them to understand and manage their emotions in response to these new situations, making it easier to adapt and thrive.

- Managing stress and maintaining well-being: Remote work and constant travel can be stressful, leading to burnout and mental health challenges. Introspection helps digital nomads become aware of their stressors and emotional states, while EI provides them with the tools to cope with these emotions effectively. This self-awareness and emotional regulation are crucial for maintaining overall well-being and preventing burnout.

- Building and maintaining relationships: Forming and maintaining personal and professional connections is vital for digital nomads, as these relationships provide social support and networking opportunities. EI helps them to empathize with others, communicate effectively, and navigate conflicts, which are essential skills for building strong relationships. Introspection, on the other hand, enables them to reflect on their interactions and learn from their experiences, fostering more meaningful connections over time.

- Decision-making and problem-solving: Digital nomads face unique challenges and must make countless decisions, from choosing their next destination to managing their work schedules. Introspection allows them to identify their values, goals, and priorities, which can guide their decision-making process. EI, in turn, helps them to consider the emotions and perspectives of others, resulting in more thoughtful and balanced decisions.

- Career growth and satisfaction: Introspection and EI contribute to digital nomads' professional development by helping them identify their strengths, weaknesses, and passions. This self-awareness can inform their career choices and lead to greater satisfaction and success in their remote work endeavours.

In conclusion, introspection and emotional intelligence are critical skills for digital nomads as they navigate the complexities of remote work and travel. Cultivating these skills can help digital nomads adapt to new environments, manage stress, build strong relationships, make informed decisions, and ultimately achieve personal and professional fulfilment.

A brief overview of the topics covered in the book and what readers can expect to learn from it.

The book covers a range of topics related to introspection, emotional intelligence, and self-discovery for digital nomads. Readers can expect to learn about:

- The definition of introspection and emotional intelligence and their significance for digital nomads.
- Self-discovery exercises, including journaling prompts, mindfulness practices, and creative expression, that can be done anywhere to increase self-awareness.
- A life planning workbook, including tips for setting achievable and realistic goals and tracking progress towards personal growth.
- Strategies for reducing distractions and staying focused on personal growth goals while on the road.
- Techniques for improving emotional intelligence, such as empathy, self-regulation, and effective communication skills.
- The benefits of introspection and emotional intelligence for personal growth, relationship building, and overall well-being.
- An understanding that the self-discovery journey is unique for each digital nomad and may take time and effort.

Overall, readers can expect to learn about the importance of introspection and emotional intelligence for personal growth and fulfilment as a digital nomad. The book provides practical tools, techniques, and strategies for self-discovery and self-awareness that can help digital nomads navigate the complexities of remote work and travel and find greater happiness and success on the road. The unique challenges and opportunities of the digital nomad lifestyle and how self-discovery and self-awareness can help

The benefits of self-discovery and self-awareness for digital nomads, including improved decision-making, better relationships, and increased resilience in the face of change

Self-discovery and self-awareness are essential aspects of personal growth and well-being, especially for digital nomads who often face unique challenges and opportunities. Developing self-discovery and self-awareness can lead to various benefits for digital nomads, including improved decision-making, better relationships, and increased resilience in the face of change.

- Improved decision-making: Self-discovery helps digital nomads understand their values, goals, and passions, which can guide them in making better decisions regarding their careers, travel destinations, and personal lives. Self-awareness enables them to recognize their strengths and weaknesses, allowing them to make informed choices and capitalize on opportunities that align with their skills and interests.

- Better relationships: Developing self-awareness allows digital nomads to recognize their communication styles, emotional patterns, and preferences, which can help them build and maintain strong personal and professional relationships. By understanding themselves better, they can communicate more effectively, empathize with others, and navigate conflicts with greater ease. This skill is particularly valuable for digital nomads who frequently encounter new people and need to establish connections quickly.

- Increased resilience in the face of change: Digital nomads often face rapid changes in their environments, work situations, and social circles. Self-discovery and self-awareness can help them cultivate emotional resilience, enabling them to adapt to new circumstances and cope with stress and uncertainty more effectively. By understanding their emotional reactions to change, digital nomads can develop healthy coping strategies and maintain their well-being, even in challenging situations.

- Enhanced personal growth: Self-discovery and self-awareness facilitate personal growth by helping digital nomads gain insights into their motivations, desires, and values. This understanding can lead to a more authentic and fulfilling life, as they can align their choices and actions with their true selves. Personal growth can also contribute to increased confidence and self-esteem, which are essential for navigating the digital nomad lifestyle.

- Greater work-life balance: As digital nomads juggle remote work and personal life; self-awareness can help them set boundaries and prioritize their well-being. By understanding their needs and recognizing when they need to step away from work or engage in self-care, digital nomads can maintain a healthier work-life balance and prevent burnout.

In conclusion, the benefits of self-discovery and self-awareness for digital nomads are numerous and far-reaching. By cultivating these skills, digital nomads can improve their decision-making, foster better relationships, and build resilience in the face of change, ultimately leading to a more satisfying and fulfilling life.

How introspection and emotional intelligence can help digital nomads to overcome common challenges such as loneliness, burnout, and lack of purpose.

Introspection and emotional intelligence (EI) are valuable tools that can help digital nomads overcome common challenges such as loneliness, burnout, and lack of purpose. By developing these skills, digital nomads can enhance their well-being and overall satisfaction with their chosen lifestyle.

- Loneliness: Loneliness can be a significant challenge for digital nomads as they frequently move and find themselves in unfamiliar environments. Introspection can help them understand their needs for connection and identify the types of relationships they value. Emotional intelligence enables them to empathize with others, communicate effectively, and build meaningful connections, which can alleviate feelings of loneliness. Additionally, EI can help digital nomads recognize when they are feeling lonely and seek social support or engage in activities that foster connection.

- Burnout: Digital nomads often face demanding workloads and struggle to maintain a healthy work-life balance, increasing the risk of burnout. Introspection allows them to reflect on their stressors, identify patterns that contribute to burnout, and develop strategies to address these issues. Emotional intelligence enables them to manage their emotions effectively, maintain self-awareness, and practice self-regulation, which can help prevent burnout. Digital nomads can also use their EI skills to set boundaries, prioritize self-care, and maintain a healthier balance between work and personal life.

- Lack of purpose: The digital nomad lifestyle may sometimes lead to feelings of aimlessness or lack of purpose. Introspection can help them identify their core values, passions, and goals, which can guide their actions and provide a sense of direction. By reflecting on their experiences and aspirations, digital nomads can align their decisions with their true selves, leading to a more purpose-driven and fulfilling life. Emotional intelligence plays a role in helping them understand and navigate their emotions associated with their sense of purpose, enabling them to make adjustments and seek opportunities that align with their values.

In summary, introspection and emotional intelligence are essential tools for digital nomads to overcome common challenges such as loneliness, burnout, and lack of purpose. By cultivating these skills, digital nomads can enhance their well-being, build meaningful connections, and find direction in their lives, ultimately leading to a more fulfilling and successful lifestyle.

Examples of successful digital nomads who have used introspection and emotional intelligence to enhance their lifestyle and achieve personal fulfillment.

There are many successful digital nomads who have used introspection and emotional intelligence to enhance their lifestyle and achieve personal fulfillment. Here are a few examples:

- Tim Ferriss is a bestselling author and entrepreneur who has used introspection and emotional intelligence to achieve success and personal fulfillment as a digital nomad. Through his writing and podcasts, he shares his insights on self-awareness, goal setting, and finding happiness and purpose in life.

- Chris Guillebeau is a bestselling author, speaker, and world traveller who has used introspection and emotional intelligence to achieve his goals and live a fulfilling life as a digital nomad. Through his writing and speaking engagements, he shares his insights on self-discovery, goal setting, and creating a meaningful life on the road.

- Nomadic Matt is a travel blogger and author who has used introspection and emotional intelligence to achieve personal fulfillment and success as a digital nomad. Through his writing and public speaking, he shares his insights on traveling, goal setting, and finding happiness and purpose in life.

These are just a few examples of digital nomads who have used introspection and emotional intelligence to enhance their lifestyle and achieve personal fulfillment. By following their examples, digital nomads can learn about the importance of self-awareness, emotional intelligence, and personal growth, and can use these tools to achieve success and fulfillment on the road.

An overview of the various self-discovery and self-awareness techniques that will be covered in the book, such as journaling, mindfulness, and creative expression.

In the book, we will cover various self-discovery and self-awareness techniques that can help digital nomads enhance their personal and professional lives. By engaging in these practices, digital nomads can better understand themselves, manage their emotions, and navigate the unique challenges of their lifestyle. Some of the techniques covered in the book include:

- Journaling: Journaling is a powerful tool for self-discovery and self-awareness. It allows individuals to record their thoughts, emotions, and experiences, providing a space for reflection and insight. In the book, we will discuss different journaling methods, such as daily gratitude journals, stream-of-consciousness writing, and prompt-based journaling, and explore how these techniques can support digital nomads in their personal growth.

- Mindfulness: Mindfulness involves cultivating present-moment awareness and acceptance of one's thoughts, emotions, and experiences. It can help digital nomads develop self-awareness and emotional intelligence, as well as reduce stress and improve overall well-being. The book will introduce various mindfulness practices, including meditation, mindful breathing, body scans, and mindful eating, and explain how to incorporate these techniques into daily life.

- Creative expression: Engaging in creative activities such as painting, writing, photography, or music can facilitate self-discovery and self-awareness by allowing individuals to explore and express their emotions, thoughts, and experiences. The book will offer guidance on how digital nomads can harness their creativity as a means of personal growth and self-understanding, including suggestions for creative projects and practices tailored to their unique lifestyle.

- Personality assessments: Personality assessments can offer insights into an individual's strengths, weaknesses, communication styles, and preferences. In the book, we will explore various assessments, such as the Myers-Briggs Type Indicator (MBTI), Enneagram, and StrengthsFinder, and discuss how digital nomads can use these tools to better understand themselves and improve their personal and professional relationships.

- Goal setting and visualization: Setting goals and visualizing desired outcomes can help digital nomads clarify their values, aspirations, and priorities. The book will cover techniques for effective goal setting and visualization, such as SMART goals, vision boards, and mental imagery exercises, and demonstrate how these practices can support self-discovery and personal growth.

- Feedback and reflection: Seeking feedback from others and engaging in self-reflection can provide valuable insights into one's behaviours, thought patterns, and emotional responses. The book will discuss strategies for soliciting constructive feedback and incorporating self-reflection into daily routines, such as conducting regular personal check-ins or participating in peer mentoring groups.

By exploring and practicing these self-discovery and self-awareness techniques, digital nomads can gain a deeper understanding of themselves, better manage their emotions, and navigate the challenges and opportunities of their unique lifestyle with greater confidence and resilience.

Understanding the connection between introspection, emotional intelligence, and personal fulfillment as a digital nomad

How introspection and emotional intelligence can lead to greater self-awareness and personal fulfillment as a digital nomad

Introspection and emotional intelligence (EI) are essential components of personal growth and well-being, especially for digital nomads who face unique challenges and opportunities. Developing these skills can lead to greater self-awareness, personal fulfillment, and overall satisfaction with their chosen lifestyle. Here's how introspection and EI can contribute to greater self-awareness and personal fulfillment for digital nomads:

- Understanding personal values and goals: Introspection involves examining one's thoughts, feelings, and experiences, which can help digital nomads identify their core values, passions, and goals. This self-awareness enables them to make more informed decisions, align their actions with their true selves, and pursue a more fulfilling and purpose-driven life.

- Emotional regulation and management: Emotional intelligence involves recognizing, understanding, and managing one's emotions and those of others. For digital nomads, developing EI can help them navigate the emotional ups and downs of their lifestyle, such as adapting to new environments, coping with loneliness, and managing stress. By effectively regulating their emotions, digital nomads can achieve greater well-being and personal fulfillment.

- Improved relationships: Greater self-awareness and emotional intelligence enable digital nomads to communicate effectively, empathize with others, and build stronger personal and professional relationships. These skills can help digital nomads establish meaningful connections, even in the face of constant change, and foster a support network that contributes to their overall satisfaction and fulfillment.

- Enhanced adaptability and resilience: Digital nomads face frequent changes in their environments, work situations, and social circles. Introspection and emotional intelligence can help them develop emotional resilience, enabling them to better adapt to new circumstances and cope with stress and uncertainty. This adaptability and resilience are crucial for achieving personal fulfillment and maintaining well-being in the face of change.

- Personal growth and development: Introspection and emotional intelligence facilitate personal growth by helping digital nomads gain insights into their motivations, desires, and values. This understanding can lead to a more authentic and fulfilling life, as they can align their choices and actions with their true selves. Personal growth can also contribute to increased confidence and self-esteem, which are essential for navigating the digital nomad lifestyle.

In conclusion, introspection and emotional intelligence can significantly contribute to greater self-awareness and personal fulfillment as a digital nomad. By cultivating these skills, digital nomads can better understand themselves, manage their emotions, and navigate the unique challenges and opportunities of their lifestyle, ultimately leading to a more satisfying and fulfilling life.

The role of introspection in helping digital nomads to identify their values, priorities, and life goals

Introspection plays a crucial role in helping digital nomads identify their values, priorities, and life goals, which is essential for living a fulfilling and purpose-driven life. The unique lifestyle of digital nomads, characterized by frequent travel, remote work, and exposure to diverse cultures and experiences, makes introspection even more important. Here's how introspection can help digital nomads in identifying their values, priorities, and life goals:

- Self-understanding: Introspection involves the examination and reflection of one's thoughts, emotions, and experiences. By engaging in regular introspective practices, digital nomads can develop a deeper understanding of themselves, including their strengths, weaknesses, preferences, and emotional patterns.

- Identifying values: Through introspection, digital nomads can identify their core values, which serve as guiding principles for their decisions and actions. By understanding what matters most to them, digital nomads can align their lifestyle choices with their values, resulting in greater satisfaction and personal fulfillment.

- Setting priorities: Introspective reflection can help digital nomads evaluate their current circumstances and prioritize different aspects of their lives, such as work, relationships, personal development, and leisure. By understanding their priorities, digital nomads can make more informed decisions about how to allocate their time and resources, ensuring that they focus on what truly matters to them.

- Establishing life goals: Introspection enables digital nomads to explore their passions, aspirations, and long-term objectives. By reflecting on their experiences and envisioning their ideal future, digital nomads can establish life goals that provide a sense of direction and purpose. These goals can serve as a roadmap for their personal and professional growth, helping them navigate the challenges and opportunities of their unique lifestyle.

- Monitoring progress and growth: Regular introspection allows digital nomads to assess their progress toward their goals, identify areas for improvement, and celebrate their achievements. By consistently evaluating their personal growth, digital nomads can stay aligned with their values, priorities, and life goals, making adjustments as needed to ensure continued satisfaction and fulfillment.

In summary, introspection is vital for digital nomads to identify their values, priorities, and life goals. By engaging in regular self-reflection and examination, digital nomads can gain a deeper understanding of themselves, align their choices with their true selves, and pursue a more fulfilling and purpose-driven life.

The impact of emotional intelligence on building meaningful relationships and creating a supportive network while on the road

Emotional intelligence (EI) is the ability to recognize, understand, and manage one's emotions and those of others. For digital nomads, who often face frequent changes in their environments and social circles, EI plays a critical role in building meaningful relationships and creating a supportive network. Here's how emotional intelligence can help digital nomads achieve this:

- Empathy and understanding: Emotional intelligence allows digital nomads to empathize with others, which is essential for forming deep connections. By understanding the feelings, needs, and perspectives of others, digital nomads can build trust, rapport, and mutual respect, fostering strong and lasting relationships.

- Effective communication: Good communication skills are a key component of emotional intelligence. Digital nomads can use their EI to express themselves clearly, listen actively, and respond appropriately to others, which is vital for maintaining healthy relationships. Effective communication also helps digital nomads navigate cultural differences and language barriers, which are common challenges while on the road.

- Conflict resolution: Emotional intelligence enables digital nomads to manage conflicts effectively by staying calm, understanding different viewpoints, and finding mutually beneficial solutions. By addressing disagreements and misunderstandings in a constructive manner, digital nomads can maintain positive relationships and prevent conflicts from escalating or causing lasting damage.

- Emotional support: A supportive network is crucial for digital nomads, who often face unique challenges such as loneliness, stress, and adapting to new environments. Emotional intelligence allows digital nomads to provide emotional support to others and seek it when needed, helping them establish a reliable and caring support system.

- Adapting to social situations: Digital nomads frequently encounter new social situations and must quickly establish connections with others. Emotional intelligence helps them adapt to different social settings, understand social cues, and respond appropriately, making it easier to form new relationships and expand their network.

- Collaboration and teamwork: Many digital nomads work remotely and collaborate with teams or clients across the globe. Emotional intelligence is essential for effective collaboration, as it enables digital nomads to understand their colleagues' emotions, communicate clearly, and resolve conflicts, ultimately contributing to a positive work environment.

In conclusion, emotional intelligence plays a significant role in building meaningful relationships and creating a supportive network for digital nomads. By developing their emotional intelligence, digital nomads can enhance their interpersonal skills, navigate the challenges of their lifestyle, and cultivate a strong support system that contributes to their overall well-being and success.

How introspection and emotional intelligence can foster resilience and adaptability in the face of change and uncertainty in the digital nomad lifestyle

Introspection and emotional intelligence (EI) can be valuable tools for digital nomads in fostering resilience and adaptability in the face of change and uncertainty. The digital nomad lifestyle often involves navigating new environments, adjusting to different cultures, and managing remote work situations. Developing introspection and emotional intelligence can help digital nomads cope with these challenges more effectively:

- Self-awareness: Introspection allows digital nomads to better understand their emotions, thought patterns, and reactions to change and uncertainty. This self-awareness is crucial for recognizing stressors, identifying personal triggers, and developing coping strategies.

- Emotional regulation: Emotional intelligence helps digital nomads manage their emotions effectively, allowing them to remain calm and focused during challenging situations. By practicing emotional regulation, digital nomads can maintain a positive outlook, reduce anxiety, and make more informed decisions when faced with change and uncertainty.

- Problem-solving: Introspection and emotional intelligence enable digital nomads to approach problems with a solution-oriented mindset, helping them assess situations objectively and identify potential solutions. This problem-solving ability contributes to their adaptability and resilience, as they can navigate challenges more effectively and bounce back from setbacks.

- Flexibility and open-mindedness: EI fosters flexibility and open-mindedness by helping digital nomads understand different perspectives and adapt to new situations. By being open to new experiences and embracing change, digital nomads can develop a greater sense of adaptability and resilience in the face of uncertainty.

- Social support: Emotional intelligence aids digital nomads in building and maintaining strong relationships, which can provide social support during challenging times. Having a supportive network can significantly contribute to resilience, as digital nomads can lean on others for emotional support, advice, and encouragement.

- Learning from experiences: Introspection allows digital nomads to reflect on their experiences and learn from them, turning challenges and setbacks into opportunities for growth. By continually learning from change and uncertainty, digital nomads can strengthen their resilience and adaptability over time.

- Confidence and self-esteem: Developing introspection and emotional intelligence can enhance digital nomads' confidence and self-esteem, allowing them to trust in their ability to handle change and uncertainty. This self-assurance contributes to their resilience and adaptability, as they can approach new situations with a positive mindset and a belief in their capacity to succeed.

In summary, introspection and emotional intelligence can significantly contribute to fostering resilience and adaptability for digital nomads in the face of change and uncertainty. By cultivating these skills, digital nomads can better understand themselves, manage their emotions, and navigate the unique challenges of their lifestyle, ultimately leading to greater success and well-being.

The importance of finding balance and meaning in the digital nomad lifestyle through introspection and emotional intelligence.

Finding balance and meaning in the digital nomad lifestyle is crucial for maintaining well-being, satisfaction, and long-term success. Introspection and emotional intelligence (EI) can help digital nomads achieve this balance and discover a deeper sense of meaning in their lives. Here's why introspection and emotional intelligence are essential for finding balance and meaning in the digital nomad lifestyle:

- Aligning values and actions: Introspection enables digital nomads to identify their core values and passions, allowing them to make choices that align with their true selves. Emotional intelligence helps them understand the emotions driving their decisions and actions. By staying true to their values and being aware of their emotions, digital nomads can lead more authentic and fulfilling lives.

- Work-life balance: Emotional intelligence can help digital nomads manage their work-related stress and maintain healthy boundaries between their professional and personal lives. By understanding and managing their emotions, digital nomads can prevent burnout, maintain productivity, and enjoy their personal time, creating a more balanced and sustainable lifestyle.

- Emotional well-being: Introspection and emotional intelligence contribute to emotional well-being by allowing digital nomads to recognize, process, and regulate their emotions effectively. By managing their emotions, they can reduce stress, anxiety, and feelings of loneliness, fostering greater overall happiness and satisfaction.

- Personal growth and self-discovery: Regular introspection and the development of emotional intelligence can lead to personal growth and self-discovery. Digital nomads can gain insights into their strengths, weaknesses, motivations, and desires, which can contribute to a deeper sense of meaning and purpose in their lives.

- Building meaningful relationships: Emotional intelligence helps digital nomads establish and maintain meaningful relationships by fostering empathy, effective communication, and conflict resolution skills. These relationships can provide emotional support, connection, and a sense of belonging, which are crucial for finding meaning and maintaining well-being in the digital nomad lifestyle.

- Adaptability and resilience: Introspection and emotional intelligence can help digital nomads develop adaptability and resilience, allowing them to navigate the uncertainties and challenges of their lifestyle more effectively. By cultivating these skills, digital nomads can maintain a sense of balance and meaning, even in the face of change and adversity.

- Mindfulness and presence: Introspection and emotional intelligence encourage mindfulness and presence, enabling digital nomads to be more engaged in their experiences and appreciate the unique opportunities their lifestyle provides. By living in the moment and appreciating their experiences, digital nomads can find deeper meaning and satisfaction in their lives.

In conclusion, introspection and emotional intelligence are essential for finding balance and meaning in the digital nomad lifestyle. By cultivating these skills, digital nomads can align their actions with their values, maintain their emotional well-being, develop meaningful relationships, and navigate the challenges and opportunities of their unique lifestyle with greater satisfaction and fulfillment.

CHAPTER 2: SELF-DISCOVERY EXERCISES FOR DIGITAL NOMADS

Journaling prompts to help you reflect on your thoughts, feelings, and experiences while traveling and working remotely

Mindfulness and meditation techniques that can be practiced anywhere to increase self-awareness and reduce stress

Mindfulness and meditation techniques can be highly beneficial for increasing self-awareness and reducing stress, especially for digital nomads who often face unique challenges and changing environments. These practices can be easily incorporated into daily routines and can be practiced anywhere. Here are some mindfulness and meditation techniques to consider:

- Mindful breathing: Focus on your breath as you inhale and exhale naturally. Pay attention to the sensation of the air entering your nostrils, filling your lungs, and then being released as you exhale. This simple practice helps you stay present and reduces stress by bringing your attention to the present moment.

- Body scan meditation: Starting at the top of your head and working your way down to your toes, mentally scan your body for any areas of tension or discomfort. As you identify these areas, consciously release the tension, and relax your muscles. This practice helps you become more aware of your body and promotes relaxation.

- Loving-kindness meditation: Focus on cultivating feelings of love, compassion, and goodwill towards yourself and others. Begin by directing these positive feelings towards yourself, then gradually extend them to loved ones, acquaintances, strangers, and eventually all beings. This practice fosters empathy, compassion, and emotional well-being.

- Walking meditation: Choose a quiet, comfortable place to walk, such as a park or a quiet street. As you walk, focus on the sensation of your feet touching the ground, the movement of your legs, and breathing. This practice helps you stay present and mindful during physical activity.

- Five senses meditation: Bring your attention to each of your five senses, one at a time, and observe the sensations associated with them. For example, notice the sounds around you, the taste in your mouth, or the feeling of the breeze on your skin. This practice helps you stay grounded and present in the moment.

- Noting thoughts and emotions: As you meditate, simply observe your thoughts and emotions as they arise, without judgment or attachment. Acknowledge their presence, then gently bring your focus back to your breath or another point of concentration. This practice increases self-awareness and helps you develop a non-judgmental relationship with your thoughts and emotions.

- Guided meditation: Use a guided meditation app or audio recording to follow along with specific instructions and visualizations, which can help you focus and maintain your meditation practice. Many guided meditations are tailored to specific goals, such as stress reduction, improved sleep, or increased self-awareness.

By incorporating these mindfulness and meditation techniques into your daily routine, you can increase self-awareness, reduce stress, and enhance overall well-being, regardless of where you are in the world. These practices are particularly beneficial for digital nomads, who often face unique challenges and need effective strategies to maintain balance and well-being in their lives.

Creative expression through art or writing to help you tap into your emotions and inner thoughts while on the go.

Creative expression through art or writing can be an effective way to tap into your emotions and inner thoughts, especially for digital nomads who are constantly on the go. Engaging in creative activities can help process emotions, increase self-awareness, and provide an outlet for self-expression. Here are some ideas for incorporating creative expression into your digital nomad lifestyle:

- Journaling: Keep a journal to record your thoughts, emotions, and experiences as you travel and work. Journaling can help you process your feelings, gain insights into your experiences, and track your personal growth. You can write in a physical notebook, on your laptop, or even through voice recording.

- Creative writing: Explore different forms of creative writing, such as poetry, short stories, or personal essays. Creative writing allows you to express your emotions, thoughts, and experiences through storytelling, metaphor, and other literary devices.

- Sketching and drawing: Carry a small sketchbook and pencils or pens with you and take the time to sketch and draw your surroundings, people you meet, or anything that captures your imagination. Drawing can help you observe your environment more closely and foster a deeper connection to the places you visit.

- Painting or watercolour: Experiment with painting or watercolour to express your emotions and experiences visually. Small travel-sized watercolour sets, and portable canvases are available, making it easy to create art on the go.

- Collage or mixed media: Collect materials from your travels, such as postcards, ticket stubs, or photographs, and create a collage or mixed media piece that captures your journey and emotions. This form of creative expression allows you to document your experiences and create tangible memories.

- Photography: Capture your experiences through photography and develop your unique perspective on the world. Photography can help you focus on the present moment and find beauty in everyday situations.

- Blogging or vlogging: Share your thoughts, emotions, and experiences through blogging or vlogging. This form of creative expression allows you to connect with others, document your journey, and reflect on your experiences while providing valuable insights to your audience.

- Music or dance: Explore your emotions and thoughts through music or dance, whether by playing an instrument, singing, or moving your body. Music and dance can be powerful forms of emotional expression and can help you process your experiences and feelings.

By engaging in creative expression while on the go, digital nomads can tap into their emotions, thoughts, and experiences in a meaningful way. These creative outlets can provide a sense of balance, self-awareness, and fulfilment, enhancing the overall digital nomad experience.

The benefits of incorporating self-discovery exercises into your daily routine as a digital nomad

Incorporating self-discovery exercises into your daily routine as a digital nomad can provide numerous benefits that contribute to personal growth, well-being, and overall life satisfaction. Here are some key benefits of engaging in self-discovery exercises:

- Increased self-awareness: Self-discovery exercises help you better understand your emotions, thoughts, strengths, weaknesses, and motivations. This increased self-awareness allows you to make more informed decisions, set realistic goals, and pursue a path that aligns with your values and passions.

- Emotional intelligence: Regular self-discovery practices can enhance your emotional intelligence by enabling you to recognize, understand, and manage your emotions effectively. This skill can improve your relationships, decision-making, and overall well-being.

- Resilience and adaptability: By understanding yourself and your reactions to various situations, you can develop greater resilience and adaptability in the face of challenges and changes. This is particularly important for digital nomads, who often experience frequent changes in their environments and circumstances.

- Stress reduction: Self-discovery exercises often promote mindfulness, presence, and emotional regulation, which can help reduce stress, anxiety, and burnout. These benefits are crucial for maintaining well-being and productivity as a digital nomad.

- Personal growth: Engaging in self-discovery exercises allows you to continually learn and grow from your experiences. This ongoing personal growth can lead to increased satisfaction, fulfilment, and a deeper sense of purpose in your life.

- Improved relationships: Self-discovery practices can enhance your interpersonal skills by fostering empathy, effective communication, and conflict resolution abilities. As a result, you can build stronger, more meaningful relationships, even as you navigate the changing social landscape of the digital nomad lifestyle.

- Goal setting and achievement: With a better understanding of yourself and your desires, you can set more meaningful and achievable goals. Self-discovery exercises can help you maintain focus and motivation, allowing you to work towards your goals more effectively.

- Work-life balance: Self-discovery exercises can help you identify your priorities and establish healthy boundaries, enabling you to achieve a better work-life balance. This balance is essential for maintaining long-term happiness and success in the digital nomad lifestyle.

In summary, incorporating self-discovery exercises into your daily routine as a digital nomad can lead to numerous benefits, including increased self-awareness, emotional intelligence, resilience, personal growth, and improved relationships. By dedicating time to self-discovery, you can enhance your well-being, satisfaction, and overall experience as a digital nomad.

Examples of self-discovery exercises that can be adapted to the unique needs and circumstances of digital nomads.

Digital nomads can adapt various self-discovery exercises to suit their unique needs and circumstances. Here are some examples of exercises that can be easily incorporated into the digital nomad lifestyle:

- Journaling: Write about your thoughts, emotions, and experiences in a journal, either in a physical notebook or digitally. You can focus on daily events, challenges, successes, or even try different journaling prompts to explore various aspects of your life.

- Personal SWOT analysis: Conduct a personal Strengths, Weaknesses, Opportunities, and Threats (SWOT) analysis to gain insights into your capabilities, areas for improvement, and potential external factors that can impact your goals.

- Gratitude practice: Create a daily gratitude list, noting the things you are grateful for in your life. This practice can help shift your focus towards the positive aspects of your experiences and cultivate a positive mindset.

- Mindfulness meditation: Practice mindfulness meditation regularly to become more present, aware of your thoughts and emotions, and develop a non-judgmental attitude towards yourself and your experiences.

- Visualization: Spend time visualizing your ideal life, including your personal and professional goals, relationships, and surroundings. This exercise can help clarify your aspirations and motivate you to work towards achieving them.

- Values assessment: Identify your core values and examine whether your current lifestyle aligns with these values. Reflect on any changes or adjustments you can make to live more authentically and true to yourself.

- Daily reflection: At the end of each day, take a few minutes to reflect on your experiences, emotions, and interactions. Consider what you learned, what you can improve, and what you are proud of. This practice can help you grow and evolve from your daily experiences.

- Goal setting and tracking: Set specific, measurable, achievable, relevant, and time-bound (SMART) goals for different areas of your life, such as personal development, career, and relationships. Regularly review and track your progress, adjusting your goals as needed.

- Networking and connecting: Attend events, workshops, or online forums related to your interests or career to meet like-minded individuals. Engaging in meaningful conversations and sharing experiences can contribute to self-discovery and personal growth.

- Creative expression: Use various forms of creative expression, such as writing, drawing, painting, or photography, to explore your emotions, thoughts, and experiences. This practice can help you process your feelings and gain insights into your inner world.

By incorporating these self-discovery exercises into your routine as a digital nomad, you can gain valuable insights into your emotions, thoughts, strengths, and weaknesses. These exercises can help you grow personally and professionally, adapt to new situations, and lead a more fulfilling and authentic life.

<u>Tips for making self-discovery exercises a regular part of your routine, even when you are on the move.</u>

Making self-discovery exercises a regular part of your routine as a digital nomad can be challenging, especially when you're constantly on the move. Here are some tips to help you incorporate self-discovery practices into your daily life:

- Schedule time for self-discovery: Dedicate a specific time each day or week for self-discovery exercises, such as journaling or meditation. By setting aside time in your calendar, you're more likely to prioritize and follow through with these practices.

- Start small: Begin with short, manageable exercises that can be easily incorporated into your daily routine. As you become more comfortable and consistent with these practices, you can gradually increase the time and effort you devote to self-discovery.

- Create a routine: Establish a daily or weekly routine that incorporates self-discovery exercises, making them a regular part of your life. This routine can provide structure and consistency, making it easier to maintain your self-discovery practices even as you move from place to place.

- Be flexible: As a digital nomad, your schedule and environment can change frequently. Be prepared to adapt your self-discovery practices to your current circumstances and stay open to trying new exercises and techniques.

- Utilize technology: Take advantage of digital tools and resources, such as mobile apps and online platforms, to support your self-discovery journey. These tools can provide guided exercises, reminders, and tracking features that can help you stay committed to your practices.

- Connect with like-minded individuals: Seek out fellow digital nomads or individuals who share your interest in self-discovery and personal growth. Connecting with others can provide motivation, accountability, and support as you work towards incorporating self-discovery exercises into your routine.

- Make self-discovery enjoyable: Choose self-discovery exercises that resonate with you and are enjoyable, as you're more likely to maintain these practices if they're personally fulfilling and engaging.

- Set realistic expectations: Understand that self-discovery is an ongoing process, and progress may be gradual. Be patient with yourself and avoid setting unrealistic expectations that may lead to frustration and discouragement.

- Reflect on your progress: Regularly review and reflect on your self-discovery journey, noting any insights, growth, or changes you've experienced. This reflection can help you stay motivated and committed to your self-discovery practices.

- Celebrate your successes: Acknowledge and celebrate your achievements and growth in self-discovery, no matter how small. Recognizing your progress can boost your motivation and reinforce the importance of maintaining these practices in your routine.

By following these tips and making self-discovery exercises a regular part of your routine, you can enhance your personal growth, well-being, and overall satisfaction as a digital nomad, even when you're on the move.

Mindfulness and meditation techniques that can be practiced anywhere to increase self-awareness

How mindfulness and meditation can help digital nomads to become more present and aware of their thoughts and feelings

Mindfulness and meditation can provide significant benefits to digital nomads by helping them become more present and aware of their thoughts and feelings. These practices encourage focusing on the present moment, fostering non-judgmental awareness of one's internal and external experiences. Here are some ways mindfulness and meditation can help digital nomads:

- Improved focus and concentration: Mindfulness and meditation practices train the mind to focus on the present moment, which can improve overall concentration and productivity. This increased focus is particularly beneficial for digital nomads who often have to adapt to new environments and workspaces.

- Reduced stress and anxiety: Engaging in mindfulness and meditation can help lower stress and anxiety levels by promoting relaxation and a sense of calm. For digital nomads, who often face uncertainties and challenges related to work and travel, these practices can be a valuable tool for managing stress.

- Emotional regulation: Mindfulness and meditation can enhance emotional intelligence by teaching individuals to become more aware of their emotions and respond to them in a healthier, more constructive manner. This increased emotional regulation can improve interpersonal relationships, decision-making, and overall well-being.

- Increased self-awareness: Practicing mindfulness and meditation can help digital nomads become more in tune with their thoughts, emotions, and bodily sensations. This heightened self-awareness can lead to more informed choices, better alignment with personal values, and a deeper understanding of one's needs and desires.

- Enhanced adaptability: By cultivating a non-judgmental awareness of the present moment, mindfulness and meditation can help digital nomads become more adaptable and open to change. This adaptability is essential for navigating the constantly shifting environments and circumstances of the digital nomad lifestyle.

- Greater resilience: Mindfulness and meditation practices can foster resilience by encouraging individuals to accept and learn from challenging situations, rather than resist or avoid them. This resilience can help digital nomads cope with the various obstacles they may encounter in their travels and work.

- Improved mental health: Regular mindfulness and meditation practices can have positive effects on overall mental health, including reducing symptoms of depression, anxiety, and burnout. These benefits can be particularly important for digital nomads who may experience isolation or increased stress.

- Better work-life balance: By promoting greater self-awareness and emotional regulation, mindfulness and meditation can help digital nomads establish and maintain a healthier work-life balance. This balance is crucial for long-term happiness and success in the digital nomad lifestyle.

Incorporating mindfulness and meditation practices into their daily routines can help digital nomads become more present and aware of their thoughts and feelings, leading to a range of benefits that enhance their overall well-being, productivity, and adaptability in their unique lifestyle.

Step-by-step instructions for incorporating mindfulness and meditation into your daily routine as a digital nomad.

Incorporating mindfulness and meditation into your daily routine as a digital nomad can be simple and adaptable to your lifestyle. Here is a step-by-step guide to help you get started:

- Choose a specific time: Identify a specific time during your day when you can dedicate a few minutes to mindfulness or meditation. It could be in the morning to start your day, during a break in your work, or before bed to unwind. Consistency is key, so try to practice at the same time each day.

- Find a comfortable space: Select a quiet, comfortable spot where you can sit or lie down without being disturbed. As a digital nomad, you may need to be flexible in finding suitable spaces, such as hotel rooms, co-working spaces, or outdoor areas like parks.

- Start with short sessions: Begin with short meditation or mindfulness sessions, such as 5 to 10 minutes. Gradually increase the duration as you become more comfortable and experienced with the practice.

- Focus on your breath: Close your eyes and bring your attention to your breath. Notice the sensation of your breath as it enters and exits your nostrils, or the rise and fall of your chest or abdomen as you inhale and exhale.

- Practice non-judgmental awareness: As thoughts, emotions, or sensations arise during your meditation or mindfulness practice, acknowledge them without judgment or attachment. Gently bring your focus back to your breath each time your mind wanders.

- Use guided meditation apps or resources: As a digital nomad, you can take advantage of technology to support your mindfulness and meditation practice. Use guided meditation apps or online resources, such as videos or podcasts, to help you develop your practice.

- Incorporate mindfulness into daily activities: Practice mindfulness throughout your day by bringing your full attention to everyday activities, such as eating, walking, or working. By becoming fully present in these moments, you can cultivate a sense of calm and focus.

- Set an intention: Before each meditation or mindfulness session, set an intention for your practice. This could be to cultivate a sense of calm, increase focus, or develop self-compassion. Reflect on your intention at the end of your practice to reinforce its importance.

- Track your progress: Keep a record of your mindfulness and meditation practice, noting the duration, your experiences, and any insights or challenges that arise. Tracking your progress can help you maintain motivation and identify patterns or areas for improvement.

- Be patient and persistent: Developing a consistent mindfulness and meditation practice takes time and patience. Be gentle with yourself and remember that progress may be gradual. Stay committed to your practice, even when you encounter obstacles or disruptions in your routine.

By following these steps and adapting them to your unique needs and circumstances, you can successfully incorporate mindfulness and meditation into your daily routine as a digital nomad, ultimately enhancing your well-being, focus, and adaptability in your ever-changing lifestyle.

The benefits of mindfulness and meditation for reducing stress, improving focus and concentration, and enhancing self-awareness

Mindfulness and meditation practices offer numerous benefits for mental and emotional well-being. By regularly engaging in these practices, individuals can experience positive changes in various aspects of their lives. Some of the key benefits of mindfulness and meditation include:

- Reduced stress: Practicing mindfulness and meditation can help lower stress levels by promoting relaxation and a sense of calm. These practices teach individuals to focus on the present moment and let go of worries or concerns about the past or future, ultimately reducing stress and anxiety.

- Improved focus and concentration: Mindfulness and meditation train the mind to maintain focus on a specific object, such as the breath, which can improve overall concentration and attention span. These practices can lead to increased productivity and better performance in tasks that require sustained focus.

- Enhanced self-awareness: Through mindfulness and meditation, individuals can develop a deeper understanding of their thoughts, emotions, and physical sensations. This heightened self-awareness can lead to more informed choices, better alignment with personal values, and a greater sense of self-compassion and understanding.

- Emotional regulation: Mindfulness and meditation can improve emotional intelligence by teaching individuals to become more aware of their emotions and respond to them in healthier, more constructive ways. This increased emotional regulation can improve interpersonal relationships, decision-making, and overall well-being.

- Increased resilience: By cultivating non-judgmental awareness and acceptance of challenging situations, mindfulness and meditation can foster resilience and the ability to cope with stressors and adversity more effectively.

- Improved mental health: Regular mindfulness and meditation practices have been associated with reduced symptoms of depression, anxiety, and burnout. These practices can contribute to overall mental health and well-being, helping individuals to navigate life's challenges more effectively.

- Better sleep quality: Mindfulness and meditation can help improve sleep quality by promoting relaxation, reducing stress, and quieting the mind. Improved sleep can contribute to better overall health and well-being.

- Enhanced creativity and problem-solving: By fostering greater mental clarity and focus, mindfulness and meditation can help enhance creativity and improve problem-solving abilities.

- Greater life satisfaction: Mindfulness and meditation practices can contribute to a greater sense of well-being, contentment, and life satisfaction. By cultivating present-moment awareness and a non-judgmental attitude towards one's experiences, individuals can develop a more positive outlook on life.

- Improved physical health: Research suggests that mindfulness and meditation practices can have positive effects on physical health, including reduced blood pressure, improved immune function, and better management of chronic pain.

Incorporating mindfulness and meditation into one's daily routine can lead to numerous benefits that improve mental, emotional, and physical well-being. These practices can be particularly helpful for individuals facing stressful situations, such as digital nomads navigating the challenges of work and travel.

Examples of self-discovery exercises that can be adapted to the unique needs and circumstances of digital nomads.

Digital nomads can adapt various self-discovery exercises to suit their unique needs and circumstances. These exercises can help them gain a deeper understanding of themselves, their values, and their goals. Here are some examples:

- Journaling: Writing in a journal can help digital nomads reflect on their experiences, emotions, and thoughts. They can use journal prompts or simply write about their day, insights, and challenges they face. Journaling can be done anywhere and at any time, making it a flexible exercise for digital nomads.

- Guided meditation or visualization: Digital nomads can practice guided meditation or visualization exercises to explore their inner selves, clarify their goals, and uncover their values. They can use meditation apps, online resources, or create their own visualizations based on their unique circumstances.

- Values clarification: Create a list of personal values and rank them in order of importance. Digital nomads can reflect on how well their current lifestyle aligns with these values and consider any changes they might need to make.

- Mind mapping: Digital nomads can create a visual representation of their thoughts, ideas, and goals using mind mapping techniques. This exercise can help them identify patterns, connections, and areas of focus.

- Strength's assessment: Identifying personal strengths can help digital nomads leverage their abilities to achieve their goals and overcome challenges. They can use online assessments, such as the VIA Character Strengths Survey or the CliftonStrengths assessment, to identify their strengths and consider how to apply them in their daily lives.

- Gratitude practice: Practicing gratitude can help digital nomads focus on the positive aspects of their lives and gain a greater appreciation for their experiences. They can maintain a gratitude journal or set aside time each day to reflect on things they're grateful for.

- Goal setting: Digital nomads can set short-term and long-term goals to guide their personal and professional growth. They can use the SMART goal-setting framework (Specific, Measurable, Achievable, Relevant, Time-bound) to create realistic and actionable goals.

- Vision board: Creating a vision board can help digital nomads visualize their goals, aspirations, and ideal lifestyle. They can use digital tools or physical materials to create a collage of images, words, and phrases that represent their dreams and ambitions.

- Personal SWOT analysis: A SWOT analysis (Strengths, Weaknesses, Opportunities, Threats) can help digital nomads assess their current situation and identify areas for growth and improvement. They can use this framework to create a personal development plan.

- Regular self-reflection: Setting aside time for regular self-reflection can help digital nomads stay in tune with their thoughts, emotions, and needs. They can use mindfulness techniques, such as deep breathing or body scanning, to stay present and connected with themselves.

By experimenting with these self-discovery exercises and adapting them to their unique needs and circumstances, digital nomads can gain valuable insights into themselves and foster personal growth as they navigate their ever-changing lifestyle.

Tips for making self-discovery exercises a regular part of your routine, even when you are on the move.

Incorporating self-discovery exercises into your routine as a digital nomad can be challenging due to the constantly changing environment and schedule. However, with some planning and flexibility, you can make these exercises a regular part of your life. Here are some tips to help you achieve this:

- Prioritize self-discovery: Recognize the importance of self-discovery exercises for your personal growth and well-being. Make them a priority and schedule them into your daily or weekly routine.

- Establish a routine: Create a consistent routine that includes self-discovery exercises. This could involve setting aside time each morning or evening for journaling, meditation, or other practices. Maintaining a routine can help create a sense of stability and continuity even when your environment is constantly changing.

- Start small: Begin with short, manageable self-discovery exercises that can be easily integrated into your daily life. As you become more comfortable with the practice, you can gradually increase the duration or complexity of the exercises.

- Be flexible: Be prepared to adapt your self-discovery routine to suit your changing circumstances. This could involve adjusting the time, location, or type of exercise, depending on your situation. Flexibility is key to maintaining a consistent practice while on the move.

- Use technology: Leverage technology to support your self-discovery practices. This could include using apps for meditation, journaling, or goal setting, or accessing online resources such as guided meditations, podcasts, or video tutorials.

- Set reminders: Use calendar alerts or smartphone reminders to help you stay on track with your self-discovery exercises. This can be especially helpful when you're in a new environment or dealing with a hectic schedule.

- Create a portable self-discovery kit: Assemble a small, portable kit containing items that support your self-discovery practice, such as a journal, pen, headphones, or a meditation cushion. Having a dedicated kit can make it easier to engage in self-discovery exercises, no matter where you are.

- Stay accountable: Share your self-discovery goals with a friend, family member, or fellow digital nomad. They can help you stay accountable and provide support and encouragement as you work towards your goals.

- Reflect on your progress: Regularly review your self-discovery practices and evaluate your progress. This can help you identify areas for improvement and celebrate your achievements.

- Be patient and persistent: Developing a consistent self-discovery routine takes time and effort. Be patient with yourself and remember that progress may be gradual. Stay committed to your practice, even when you encounter obstacles or disruptions in your routine.

By implementing these tips and adapting them to your unique needs and circumstances, you can successfully incorporate self-discovery exercises into your routine as a digital nomad, ultimately enhancing your personal growth and well-being in your ever-changing lifestyle.

Creative expression through art or writing to help you tap into your emotions and inner thoughts while on the go

The role of creative expression in self-discovery and personal growth for digital nomads

Creative expression plays a significant role in self-discovery and personal growth for digital nomads. Engaging in creative activities can help digital nomads explore their thoughts, emotions, and experiences while fostering a deeper understanding of themselves. Creative expression can manifest in various forms, such as writing, painting, drawing, photography, music, dance, or crafting. Here are some ways creative expression can support self-discovery and personal growth for digital nomads:

- Emotional processing: Creative expression provides an outlet for processing and expressing emotions, which can be especially helpful when dealing with the challenges and changes associated with the digital nomad lifestyle. By engaging in creative activities, digital nomads can gain insights into their emotional states and work through difficult feelings.

- Mindfulness and presence: Creative activities often require focus and presence, which can help digital nomads cultivate mindfulness and become more attuned to their thoughts and feelings. This increased self-awareness can contribute to personal growth and a better understanding of their needs and desires.

- Self-reflection: Creative expression encourages self-reflection by providing a means to explore personal experiences, beliefs, and values. Through their creative work, digital nomads can gain insights into their inner worlds, which can inform their personal growth and development.

- Building resilience: Engaging in creative expression can help digital nomads build resilience by providing a constructive way to cope with challenges and setbacks. Creative activities can serve as a form of self-care and stress relief, allowing digital nomads to recharge and maintain their well-being.

- Developing skills and talents: Pursuing creative interests can help digital nomads develop new skills and talents or refine existing ones. This personal growth can contribute to increased confidence, self-esteem, and a sense of accomplishment.

- Connection and communication: Creative expression can facilitate connections with others by providing a means to share experiences, thoughts, and emotions. This can help digital nomads build relationships and create a sense of community, even when they are far from home.

- Exploration of identity: Creative activities offer an opportunity for digital nomads to explore and express their evolving identities as they navigate their ever-changing environments and experiences. This can help them better understand their sense of self and cultivate a more authentic and fulfilling lifestyle.

- Sense of purpose: Engaging in creative expression can provide digital nomads with a sense of purpose and direction. By pursuing their creative passions, they can create a more meaningful and satisfying life experience.

- Problem-solving and innovation: Creative expression encourages divergent thinking and the ability to approach problems from multiple perspectives. This can help digital nomads develop innovative solutions to the challenges they face in their work and personal lives.

- Cultural exploration and learning: For digital nomads, creative expression can be a way to engage with and learn from the diverse cultures they encounter during their travels. This cultural exploration can foster personal growth and expand their understanding of the world.

By incorporating creative expression into their lives, digital nomads can facilitate self-discovery, personal growth, and emotional well-being while embracing the unique challenges and opportunities of their nomadic lifestyle.

Examples of creative expression techniques such as journaling, painting, drawing, or writing

Creative expression techniques can take many forms and can be tailored to individual preferences and circumstances. Here are some examples of techniques in journaling, painting, drawing, and writing that can help foster self-discovery and personal growth:

Journaling:
- Stream of consciousness writing: Write down your thoughts as they come to you, without editing or censoring yourself. This can help you access your inner thoughts and emotions.
- Gratitude journal: Record things you are grateful for each day to cultivate a positive mindset and appreciate the good in your life.
- Art journal: Combine words and images to create a visual diary that captures your thoughts, emotions, and experiences.

Painting:
- Abstract painting: Express your emotions through colours, shapes, and textures without focusing on creating a realistic image.
- Plein air painting: Paint outdoors, capturing the beauty of your surroundings and immersing yourself in the environment.
- Intuitive painting: Let go of expectations and paint spontaneously, allowing your intuition to guide your brushstrokes.

Drawing:
- Mindful doodling: Engage in spontaneous, free form drawing without focusing on the end result. This can help you relax and stay present.
- Zentangle: Create intricate, structured patterns using repetitive lines and shapes to promote focus and concentration.
- Sketch journal: Carry a small sketchbook with you to capture your observations and experiences in visual form as you travel.

Writing:
- Freewriting: Set a timer and write continuously without stopping, allowing your thoughts to flow freely onto the page.
- Creative writing prompts: Use prompts to inspire short stories, poems, or essays that help you explore your thoughts, feelings, and experiences.
- Travel writing: Document your travel experiences and share your unique perspective on the places you visit, the people you meet, and the cultures you encounter.

Other creative expression techniques that can be explored include photography, music composition, dance, and crafting (e.g., knitting, pottery, or collage-making). By experimenting with these creative techniques, individuals can discover which methods resonate with them and provide the most benefit for self-discovery and personal growth.

The benefits of creative expression for digital nomads, including stress relief, improved mood, and increased self-awareness

Creative expression offers numerous benefits for digital nomads, making it an essential tool for self-discovery, personal growth, and well-being. Here are some key benefits of engaging in creative activities:

- Stress relief: Creative expression can provide an effective outlet for stress, as it allows digital nomads to focus on the present moment and forget about their worries. By engaging in creative activities, they can experience a sense of relaxation and calmness.

- Improved mood: Creative expression can enhance mood and promote feelings of happiness and satisfaction. Participating in creative activities can trigger the release of dopamine, a neurotransmitter associated with pleasure and reward, leading to an improved sense of well-being.

- Increased self-awareness: Engaging in creative expression can help digital nomads gain a better understanding of their thoughts, emotions, and experiences. This self-awareness can lead to personal growth and a deeper sense of self.

- Enhanced problem-solving skills: Creative activities often involve thinking outside the box, encouraging digital nomads to develop innovative solutions to challenges. This can be particularly beneficial in their work and personal lives, as they face unique obstacles and adapt to new environments.

- Emotional expression: Creative expression provides an opportunity for digital nomads to process and express their emotions, helping them understand and cope with their feelings more effectively.

- Connection and communication: Through creative expression, digital nomads can share their experiences, thoughts, and emotions with others, fostering connections and building a sense of community, even when far from home.

- Personal growth: By exploring their creativity, digital nomads can discover new interests, passions, and talents, leading to personal growth and a more fulfilling life.

- Increased focus and concentration: Creative activities often require attention and presence, helping digital nomads improve their focus and concentration.

- Sense of accomplishment: Completing a creative project can provide digital nomads with a sense of accomplishment and pride, boosting their self-esteem and confidence.

- Cultural exploration: Engaging in creative expression can offer digital nomads a unique way to interact with and learn from the diverse cultures they encounter during their travels. This can foster personal growth and a broader understanding of the world.

By incorporating creative expression into their lives, digital nomads can not only enhance their well-being but also foster personal growth and self-discovery, ultimately contributing to a more fulfilling and balanced lifestyle.

Guided mindfulness and meditation exercises that can be done anywhere, even when you are on the move.

Guided mindfulness and meditation exercises can be an effective way for digital nomads to reduce stress, increase self-awareness, and cultivate a sense of inner calm, even when on the move. Here are some exercises that can be done anywhere:

Three-Minute Breathing Space: This short meditation is designed to help you reconnect with your breath and body in a brief, focused period.
- Minute 1: Close your eyes and take a few deep breaths. Focus on the sensations of your breath entering and leaving your body.
- Minute 2: Bring awareness to your body, noticing any physical sensations or tension.
- Minute 3: Expand your awareness to your surroundings, listening to the sounds and feeling the air around you.

Body Scan Meditation: This meditation helps you develop awareness of your body and any sensations or tension that may be present.
- Find a comfortable seated or lying position.
- Close your eyes and take a few deep breaths.
- Begin at the top of your head and slowly scan down through your body, bringing attention to any sensations or tension in each area.
- As you scan, release any tension, and imagine your breath flowing into and out of each body part.

Mindful Walking: This exercise can be done while walking outdoors or even pacing in a small space.
- Begin walking at a slow, comfortable pace.
- Focus on the sensations of your feet hitting the ground, the movement of your legs, and the rhythm of your breath.
- If your mind wanders, gently bring your attention back to the sensations of walking.

Loving-Kindness Meditation: This meditation promotes feelings of compassion and love for yourself and others.
- Find a comfortable seated position and close your eyes.
- Silently repeat phrases such as, "May I be happy, may I be healthy, may I be safe, may I be at ease."
- After a few minutes, shift your focus to someone you care about, repeating the phrases for them.
- Gradually extend your loving-kindness meditation to include others, such as acquaintances, strangers, and even those you may have difficulty with.

Five Senses Meditation: This exercise helps you become more present and aware of your surroundings.
- Find a comfortable seated position and close your eyes.
- Focus on each of your senses one at a time (sight, sound, smell, taste, and touch).
- Spend about one minute on each sense, observing any sensations without judgment or attachment.
- After completing all five senses, take a few deep breaths and open your eyes.

These guided mindfulness and meditation exercises can be adapted to suit your needs and circumstances, making them an accessible and valuable tool for maintaining well-being and self-awareness while on the move as a digital nomad.

Tips for making mindfulness and meditation a regular part of your routine, even in challenging or unfamiliar environments.

Incorporating mindfulness and meditation into your daily routine as a digital nomad can be challenging, especially when faced with unfamiliar environments and busy schedules. However, with a little dedication and planning, it is possible to make these practices a regular part of your life. Here are some tips to help you establish a consistent mindfulness and meditation routine:

- Set realistic goals: Start with short meditation sessions of 5-10 minutes and gradually increase the duration as you become more comfortable with the practice. Setting realistic goals will make it easier to maintain consistency and prevent discouragement.

- Create a routine: Choose a specific time of day to practice mindfulness or meditation, such as first thing in the morning, during a midday break, or before bedtime. Incorporating your practice into a daily routine can help create a habit and make it easier to remember.

- Find a designated space: While you may not always have access to a quiet, private space, try to find a consistent spot where you can practice meditation without distractions. This could be a corner of your room, a nearby park, or even your vehicle.

- Use guided meditations or apps: Guided meditation recordings or meditation apps can be helpful for staying on track and maintaining consistency in your practice. These resources often offer a variety of meditations, allowing you to choose one that suits your needs and preferences.

- Be adaptable: As a digital nomad, your environment and schedule can change frequently. Be prepared to adapt your mindfulness and meditation practice to your circumstances, such as practicing at different times of the day or finding new spaces to meditate.

- Start small and build up: If you're new to mindfulness or meditation, begin with simple exercises, such as focusing on your breath or engaging in mindful walking. As you become more comfortable with these practices, you can gradually explore more advanced techniques.

- Stay accountable: Share your mindfulness and meditation goals with a friend or join an online community of like-minded individuals. This can help you stay motivated and provide support when faced with challenges.

- Be patient and compassionate: It's normal to encounter obstacles in your mindfulness and meditation practice, such as a wandering mind or difficulty finding a quiet space. Approach these challenges with patience and self-compassion, recognizing that it's all part of the learning process.

- Incorporate mindfulness into daily activities: Practice mindfulness during everyday tasks, such as washing dishes, brushing your teeth, or walking to the store. By bringing awareness to these activities, you can cultivate mindfulness throughout your day.

- Track your progress: Keep a journal or use an app to track your mindfulness and meditation practice, noting the duration, type of meditation, and any insights or challenges you encounter. This can help you recognize your progress and maintain motivation.

By following these tips and remaining committed to your practice, you can make mindfulness and meditation a regular part of your routine, even in challenging or unfamiliar environments as a digital nomad.

Creative expression through art or writing to help you tap into your emotions and inner thoughts while on the go

The role of creative expression in self-discovery and personal growth for digital nomads

Creative expression plays a significant role in self-discovery and personal growth for digital nomads. By engaging in various creative activities, digital nomads can reap a variety of benefits that contribute to their overall well-being and personal development:

- Self-expression: Creative activities offer an outlet for digital nomads to express their thoughts, emotions, and experiences. By exploring different creative mediums, they can gain a deeper understanding of their inner selves and develop a stronger sense of identity.

- Emotional processing: Creative expression can help digital nomads process complex emotions and experiences, providing a means to cope with challenging situations, such as adjusting to new environments or dealing with feelings of loneliness and isolation.

- Mindfulness and presence: Engaging in creative activities often requires focus and presence, helping digital nomads to become more mindful and present in their daily lives. This can enhance their self-awareness and emotional intelligence.

- Stress relief: Creative expression can provide a therapeutic outlet for stress, enabling digital nomads to experience relaxation and a sense of calm in the midst of their busy, often unpredictable lives.

- Cognitive flexibility: Creative activities often involve thinking outside the box, helping digital nomads to develop cognitive flexibility and problem-solving skills. This can be particularly beneficial in their work and personal lives, as they face unique challenges and adapt to new situations.

- Building connections: Through creative expression, digital nomads can connect with others who share similar interests or experiences, creating a sense of community and belonging even when far from home.

- Cultural exploration: Engaging in creative activities can offer digital nomads a unique way to interact with and learn from the diverse cultures they encounter during their travels. By immersing themselves in local art, music, or crafts, they can develop a broader understanding of the world and foster personal growth.

- Personal growth and development: By exploring their creativity and discovering new interests, passions, and talents, digital nomads can experience personal growth and develop a more fulfilling, well-rounded life.

- Confidence building: Creative expression can help digital nomads build confidence in their abilities and provide a sense of accomplishment, which can spill over into other aspects of their lives, including work and personal relationships.

By incorporating creative expression into their daily lives, digital nomads can foster self-discovery, personal growth, and a greater sense of well-being, ultimately contributing to a more balanced and fulfilling lifestyle.

Examples of creative expression techniques such as journaling, painting, drawing, or writing

Creative expression techniques encompass a wide range of activities that can help digital nomads explore their thoughts, emotions, and experiences. Here are some examples of creative expression techniques that can be adapted to suit individual preferences and circumstances:

- Journaling: Writing daily reflections or thoughts in a journal can be a powerful way to process emotions, gain insights, and document experiences. Types of journaling include gratitude journaling, dream journaling, or travel journaling.

- Creative writing: Engaging in creative writing, such as poetry, short stories, or personal essays, can provide an outlet for self-expression and imagination. Writing prompts or participation in writing groups can help spark inspiration.

- Painting or drawing: Visual art techniques like painting or drawing can be a therapeutic way to express emotions and ideas without the need for words. Experimenting with different mediums, such as watercolour, acrylic, charcoal, or pastels, can offer a range of creative possibilities.

- Collage or mixed media: Combining various materials, such as magazine cut-outs, photographs, fabric, or found objects, to create a collage or mixed media artwork can be a unique and engaging form of creative expression.

- Photography: Capturing moments, experiences, or emotions through photography can be a powerful way to document your journey and express your creative vision. Exploring different styles and techniques, such as street photography, landscape photography, or portrait photography, can provide diverse opportunities for self-expression.

- Digital art: Creating digital artwork using graphic design software or drawing tablets can offer a modern and portable form of creative expression that is well-suited to the digital nomad lifestyle.

- Music or song writing: Playing an instrument, singing, or composing original songs can be a deeply personal and rewarding form of creative expression. Many digital nomads find solace and inspiration in music, which can also serve as a way to connect with others.

- Dance or movement: Engaging in dance or movement practices, such as yoga, tai chi, or contemporary dance, can provide a physical and emotional outlet for creative expression, helping digital nomads to connect with their bodies and emotions.

- Handcrafts: Knitting, crocheting, sewing, or embroidery can be meditative forms of creative expression that also result in tangible creations. Handcrafts can be easily carried along during travels and provide a relaxing break from screen time.

- Cooking or baking: Experimenting with new recipes or creating original dishes inspired by local ingredients and culinary traditions can be a delicious and creative way to immerse yourself in the culture of the places you visit.

These creative expression techniques can be adapted and combined to suit individual preferences and circumstances, providing digital nomads with diverse opportunities for self-discovery, personal growth, and emotional well-being.

The benefits of creative expression for digital nomads, including stress relief, improved mood, and increased self-awareness

Creative expression offers numerous benefits for digital nomads, contributing to their overall well-being and personal growth. Some of the key benefits include:

- Stress relief: Engaging in creative activities can help reduce stress by providing a focused, meditative outlet for the mind. Creative expression can offer a respite from daily challenges and promote relaxation.

- Improved mood: Creative activities stimulate the production of feel-good chemicals in the brain, such as dopamine and serotonin, which can improve mood and increase feelings of happiness and satisfaction.

- Increased self-awareness: Creative expression allows digital nomads to explore their thoughts, emotions, and experiences, fostering greater self-awareness and understanding of their inner selves.

- Emotional processing: Creative activities can help digital nomads process complex emotions, providing a healthy outlet for self-expression and emotional release.

- Enhanced cognitive function: Creative expression can help improve cognitive function by stimulating neural connections in the brain, enhancing problem-solving skills, critical thinking, and adaptability.

- Personal growth and development: Through creative exploration, digital nomads can gain new insights, learn new skills, and develop a stronger sense of identity, contributing to personal growth and development.

- Building connections: Creative expression can help digital nomads connect with others who share similar interests, fostering a sense of community and belonging even when far from home.

- Cultural exploration: Engaging in creative activities inspired by the diverse cultures encountered during travels can provide a unique way for digital nomads to learn from and connect with the local communities, enhancing personal growth and understanding.

- Increased focus and concentration: Many creative activities require sustained focus and attention, helping to improve concentration and mindfulness.

- Boosted self-esteem and confidence: Creative expression can provide a sense of accomplishment and pride in one's abilities, resulting in increased self-esteem and confidence, which can positively impact other areas of a digital nomad's life.

By incorporating creative expression into their daily lives, digital nomads can experience a range of benefits that contribute to their overall well-being, personal growth, and fulfilment while navigating the unique challenges and opportunities of their lifestyle.

Step-by-step instructions for incorporating creative expression into your daily routine as a digital nomad.

Incorporating creative expression into your daily routine as a digital nomad can help improve your overall well-being and personal growth. Follow these step-by-step instructions to make creative activities a regular part of your lifestyle:

- Identify your creative interests: Begin by exploring different forms of creative expression, such as painting, drawing, writing, photography, music, or dance. Consider which activities resonate most with you and align with your skills, interests, and available resources.

- Set realistic goals: Start with small, achievable goals that can be easily incorporated into your daily routine. For example, you might commit to spending 15 minutes per day on creative writing or sketching.

- Create a routine: Schedule a specific time each day to engage in your chosen creative activity. Consistency is key to establishing a routine, so try to stick to the same time each day, whether it's first thing in the morning, during a lunch break, or before bedtime.

- Prepare your creative space: Set up a dedicated space for your creative activities, even if it's just a small corner of your room or a portable art kit that you can take with you. Having a designated space can help signal to your brain that it's time to focus on your creative practice.

- Use prompts or inspiration: If you're struggling to find inspiration or ideas for your creative activities, consider using prompts or seeking inspiration from your surroundings. For example, you might use writing prompts, follow a drawing challenge, or take photographs of interesting architecture or landscapes you encounter during your travels.

- Stay accountable: Share your creative goals with a friend or join an online community of like-minded individuals who can offer support and encouragement. By staying accountable to others, you'll be more likely to maintain your creative routine.

- Be adaptable: As a digital nomad, your environment and schedule can change frequently. Be prepared to adapt your creative routine to your circumstances, such as practicing at different times of the day, using different materials, or finding new sources of inspiration.

- Track your progress: Keep a journal or use an app to track your creative activities, noting the time spent, type of activity, and any insights or challenges you encounter. Tracking your progress can help you recognize your achievements and maintain motivation.

- Prioritize self-care: Ensure that you're getting adequate rest, nutrition, and exercise to support your overall well-being and creative energy. Self-care is essential for maintaining a sustainable creative routine.

- Be patient and compassionate: It's normal to experience setbacks, lack of inspiration, or frustration in your creative practice. Approach these challenges with patience and self-compassion, recognizing that they are part of the creative process, and that growth takes time.

By following these steps and remaining committed to your creative practice, you can successfully incorporate creative expression into your daily routine as a digital nomad, ultimately enhancing your overall well-being and personal growth.

Examples of how to make creative expression a regular part of your routine, even when you are on the move.

Making creative expression a regular part of your routine while on the move can be challenging, but it's possible with a bit of planning, flexibility, and determination. Here are some examples of how to incorporate creative expression into your daily life as a digital nomad:

- Portable materials: Invest in portable and compact art supplies or creative tools that are easy to carry and use while traveling. For instance, a small sketchbook, travel watercolour set, or a compact writing notebook can be carried in your backpack or purse for quick access.

- Digital tools: Utilize digital tools and apps for creative activities, such as digital drawing tablets, writing apps, or music composition software. These tools can be easily accessed on your laptop, tablet, or smartphone, making them convenient for on-the-go creativity.

- Set aside time: Designate a specific time each day for creative activities, such as during your morning coffee, while waiting for transportation, or before bed. Consistency is key to establishing a routine, so try to maintain the same timeframe each day, even when you're on the move.

- Use your surroundings as inspiration: Draw inspiration from your surroundings to fuel your creative expression. Write about your experiences, sketch local landmarks, or capture photographs of the landscapes you encounter.

- Practice micro-creativity: Engage in short bursts of creativity throughout the day, such as jotting down a few lines of poetry, sketching a quick doodle, or brainstorming ideas for a short story.

These micro-creative sessions can help keep your creative momentum going, even when you're short on time.

- Connect with local creatives: Attend workshops, classes, or meetups in the locations you visit to connect with local creative communities. This can provide inspiration, support, and opportunities for collaboration, helping to maintain your creative routine while traveling.

- Embrace imperfection: Accept that your creative routine might not always be perfect while on the move. Focus on the process rather than the outcome and allow yourself the flexibility to adapt and experiment with different creative practices.

- Document your journey: Use creative expression as a means to document your travels and experiences. This can help you maintain a sense of purpose and motivation in your creative routine, even when you're on the move.

- Set creative goals: Establish specific creative goals for your travels, such as completing a series of drawings, writing a collection of travel essays, or creating a photo series. Having a clear goal can help you stay focused and committed to your creative routine.

- Combine creativity with relaxation: Pair your creative activities with relaxation or self-care practices, such as practicing mindfulness while sketching, writing in a journal before bedtime, or painting while listening to calming music.

By incorporating these strategies into your daily routine, you can maintain a consistent creative practice even as a digital nomad on the move. Remember to be flexible, patient, and open to new experiences and inspiration along your journey.

<u>Tips for staying motivated and inspired to continue your creative expression practice as a digital nomad.</u>

Maintaining motivation and inspiration for creative expression as a digital nomad can be challenging due to the dynamic nature of the lifestyle. Here are some tips to help you stay inspired and motivated:

- Set clear goals: Establish specific, achievable creative goals to give your practice direction and purpose. Break down larger goals into smaller, manageable steps to track progress and maintain motivation.

- Schedule time for creativity: Consistently dedicate time in your daily or weekly schedule for creative activities. Prioritize and protect this time to ensure that it becomes a regular part of your routine.

- Connect with others: Join online forums, social media groups, or local meetups to connect with fellow digital nomads or creative individuals. Sharing your work, discussing ideas, and collaborating with others can help keep you motivated and inspired.

- Seek new inspiration: Regularly expose yourself to new experiences, cultures, and environments to stimulate your creativity. Attend events, visit galleries or museums, or explore local landmarks to gather new ideas and inspiration.

- Document your progress: Keep a journal or digital log to track your creative journey, noting accomplishments, challenges, and insights. Reflecting on your progress can help boost motivation and maintain a sense of purpose.

- Embrace imperfection: Accept that your creative practice may not always be perfect, especially while traveling. Focus on the process rather than the outcome and allow yourself the freedom to experiment and make mistakes.

- Stay accountable: Share your creative goals with friends, family, or an online community to maintain accountability. Regular check-ins or updates on your progress can help keep you motivated and committed to your practice.

- Set realistic expectations: Acknowledge the limitations of your lifestyle and adjust your creative expectations accordingly. Be patient with yourself and celebrate small victories along the way.

- Engage in continuous learning: Invest in your creative development by taking workshops, courses, or tutorials to expand your skills and knowledge. Continuous learning can help keep your creative practice fresh and engaging.

- Practice self-care: Ensure that you are getting enough rest, proper nutrition, and exercise to support your overall well-being and creative energy. Taking care of your physical and mental health is crucial to maintaining a sustainable creative practice.

By incorporating these tips into your routine, you can foster motivation and inspiration for your creative expression practice as a digital nomad, helping you stay engaged and committed to your personal growth and well-being.

CHAPTER 3: LIFE PLANNING WORKBOOK FOR DIGITAL NOMADS

A step-by-step guide to creating a life plan that aligns with your priorities, values, and goals as a digital nomad

A collection of prompts and exercises to help you identify what is most important to you and what you want to achieve in life while on the road

Prompts and exercises can help you reflect on your values, priorities, and goals as a digital nomad. Here is a collection of activities to assist you in identifying what is most important to you and what you want to achieve in life while on the road:

- Core values exercise: Make a list of your top 10 core values, such as freedom, connection, creativity, or adventure. Reflect on how these values are currently reflected in your life and how they can guide your decision-making while traveling.

- Vision board: Create a vision board that visually represents your goals and aspirations. Include images, quotes, or words that resonate with you and symbolize what you want to achieve in life. Regularly review your vision board to keep your goals at the forefront of your mind.

- Gratitude journal: Spend a few minutes each day writing down three things you are grateful for. Focusing on gratitude can help you appreciate the positive aspects of your life and clarify what is truly important to you.

- The perfect day exercise: Write a detailed description of your ideal day, from the moment you wake up to when you go to bed. Include specifics about where you are, what you're doing, who you're with, and how you feel. This exercise can help you identify the elements that contribute to your happiness and fulfillment.

- Goal-setting worksheet: Create a worksheet that outlines your short-term, medium-term, and long-term goals in various aspects of your life, such as career, relationships, health, and personal growth. Break each goal down into actionable steps and set deadlines to keep yourself accountable.

- Mind maps: Use mind maps to explore different areas of your life and generate ideas for what you want to achieve. Start with a central theme (e.g., career, relationships, or personal growth) and branch out with related ideas and goals.

- The "why" exercise: For each of your goals or aspirations, ask yourself "why" you want to achieve them. Continue asking "why" for each response until you reach the core motivation behind your goal. This exercise can help you determine if your goals align with your values and priorities.

- Letter to your future self: Write a letter to your future self, outlining your hopes, dreams, and goals for the next five to ten years. Be specific about what you want to achieve and the person you hope to become. Revisit the letter periodically to assess your progress and re-evaluate your goals.

- Reverse bucket list: Create a list of accomplishments, experiences, or moments in your life that you are proud of or grateful for. Reflecting on your past achievements can help you identify patterns and themes that are important to you and guide your future goals.

- Personal SWOT analysis: Conduct a personal SWOT analysis by listing your strengths, weaknesses, opportunities, and threats. This exercise can help you gain self-awareness and develop strategies to leverage your strengths, address your weaknesses, and pursue opportunities while mitigating threats.

By engaging in these prompts and exercises, you can gain insight into your values, priorities, and goals as a digital nomad, helping you create a fulfilling life on the road that aligns with your deepest desires and aspirations.

Tips for setting achievable and realistic goals and tracking your progress towards your dreams while traveling and working remotely.

Setting achievable and realistic goals while traveling and working remotely can be challenging, but it's essential for maintaining motivation and staying on track. Here are some tips for setting goals and tracking your progress as a digital nomad:

- Set SMART goals: Make your goals Specific, Measurable, Achievable, Relevant, and Time-bound. This approach can help ensure your goals are clear, realistic, and trackable.

- Break down goals into smaller tasks: Divide larger goals into smaller, manageable tasks that can be accomplished within a shorter time frame. This can make your goals feel more achievable and provide a sense of accomplishment as you complete each task.

- Prioritize your goals: Determine which goals are most important or urgent and focus on those first. This can help you stay focused and avoid becoming overwhelmed by trying to tackle too many goals at once.

- Create a timeline: Establish a timeline for achieving your goals, with specific milestones and deadlines. This can help you stay on track and maintain a sense of progress and momentum.

- Monitor your progress: Regularly review your goals and evaluate your progress. Adjust your approach or timeline if necessary and celebrate your successes along the way.

- Stay accountable: Share your goals with friends, family, or an online community to maintain accountability. Regular check-ins or updates on your progress can help keep you motivated and committed to your goals.

- Be flexible: Accept that your goals or priorities may change as you travel and work remotely. Be willing to adapt your goals to accommodate new experiences, opportunities, or challenges.

- Use goal-setting tools: Utilize digital tools, apps, or physical planners to help you set, track, and manage your goals. These tools can help you stay organized and monitor your progress more easily.

- Reflect on your goals: Regularly reflect on your goals and the reasons behind them. This can help you stay connected to your purpose and maintain motivation throughout your journey.

- Practice self-compassion: Recognize that setbacks and obstacles are a natural part of the goal-setting process. Be kind to yourself and maintain a growth mindset, understanding that mistakes and challenges can provide valuable learning experiences.

By following these tips, you can set achievable and realistic goals while traveling and working remotely, helping you stay focused, motivated, and on track towards your dreams.

<u>The importance of regularly reviewing and updating your life plan as a digital nomad to reflect your evolving priorities, values, and goals</u>

Regularly reviewing and updating your life plan as a digital nomad is essential to ensure that your lifestyle continues to align with your evolving priorities, values, and goals. As you travel and work remotely, you may encounter new experiences, challenges, and opportunities that can shift your perspective and influence your aspirations. Here are some reasons why it's crucial to reassess your life plan:

- Personal growth: Traveling and working remotely can lead to significant personal growth and self-discovery. Regularly reviewing your life plan can help you incorporate new insights and realizations into your overall vision for your life.

- Changing priorities: Your priorities may change over time due to various factors, such as personal experiences, relationships, or career developments. Updating your life plan allows you to re-evaluate and adjust your goals to better align with your current priorities.

- Staying focused: Regularly reassessing your life plan can help you stay focused on your goals and make informed decisions that support your long-term vision, even amidst the distractions and uncertainties of the digital nomad lifestyle.

- Adapting to new circumstances: Life as a digital nomad can be unpredictable, with unexpected changes in work, relationships, or travel plans. Regularly reviewing your life plan can help you adapt to these changes and adjust your goals accordingly.

- Maintaining motivation: Revisiting your life plan can reignite your motivation and passion for your goals, especially during challenging or stagnant periods.

- Staying aligned with values: As you grow and evolve, your values may also shift. Regularly reviewing your life plan ensures that your goals and actions continue to align with your core values, promoting greater overall fulfillment and satisfaction.

- Recognizing achievements: Updating your life plan provides an opportunity to recognize and celebrate your accomplishments, boosting your confidence and motivation to continue pursuing your goals.

- Identifying new opportunities: As you travel and work remotely, you may encounter new opportunities for personal, professional, or creative growth. Regularly reviewing your life plan can help you identify and pursue these opportunities in line with your overall vision.

- Maintaining balance: A well-rounded life plan considers various aspects of your life, such as work, relationships, health, and personal growth. Regularly reassessing your plan can help you maintain balance and ensure that you're not neglecting any critical areas.

- Enhancing self-awareness: The process of reviewing and updating your life plan can deepen your self-awareness, helping you understand your evolving needs, desires, and aspirations more clearly.

By regularly reviewing and updating your life plan as a digital nomad, you can ensure that your lifestyle remains aligned with your evolving priorities, values, and goals, fostering greater fulfillment and satisfaction on your journey.

Examples of successful digital nomads who have used life planning to enhance their lifestyle and achieve personal fulfillment

Many successful digital nomads have used life planning to enhance their lifestyles and achieve personal fulfillment. Here are a few examples:

- Chris Guillebeau: Chris is an entrepreneur, author, and traveller who visited every country in the world before turning 35. Through careful planning and goal setting, he has built a successful online business and authored multiple books, including "The Art of Non-Conformity" and "The $100 Startup." Chris's life plan emphasizes personal freedom, meaningful work, and a commitment to lifelong learning.

- Pieter Levels: Pieter is a successful entrepreneur and the founder of Nomad List, a popular platform for digital nomads to find the best places to live and work remotely. By setting clear goals and priorities, Pieter has built a thriving online business while traveling the world and living a location-independent lifestyle.

- Caz and Craig Makepeace: This Australian couple, founders of the popular travel blog "Y Travel Blog," have successfully combined their love for travel with their desire to create a sustainable income and provide a fulfilling life for their children. Through careful planning, goal setting, and prioritization, they have built a successful online business that allows them to travel extensively and share their experiences with others.

- Natalie Sisson: Known as "The Suitcase Entrepreneur," Natalie has built a successful online business teaching others how to create location-independent businesses. By incorporating life planning and setting clear goals, she has achieved personal fulfillment through her work, travel, and personal growth.

- Matt Kepnes: Matt, also known as "Nomadic Matt," is a successful travel blogger, author, and entrepreneur. He set a goal to travel the world and make it his lifestyle, and through careful planning and persistence, he has built a thriving online business and authored a best-selling book, "How to Travel the World on $50 a Day."

These successful digital nomads serve as examples of how life planning can help individuals create a fulfilling lifestyle that aligns with their values and goals. By setting clear priorities, establishing goals, and regularly reviewing and updating their life plans, they have achieved personal fulfillment and success in their location-independent lifestyles.

How the life planning workbook can help digital nomads to clarify their purpose, find direction, and stay motivated while on the move.

A life planning workbook can be an invaluable tool for digital nomads, helping them clarify their purpose, find direction, and stay motivated while on the move. Here are some ways a life planning workbook can provide support and guidance for digital nomads:

- Goal setting: A workbook can help digital nomads set clear, achievable goals that align with their values and priorities. By breaking down larger objectives into smaller tasks and milestones, digital nomads can maintain a sense of direction and progress, even when facing the uncertainties and distractions of life on the road.

- Purpose clarification: A life planning workbook can guide digital nomads through exercises and reflections to help them identify their core values, passions, and purpose. This clarity can serve as a foundation for setting meaningful goals and making intentional decisions that align with their authentic selves.

- Self-awareness: Regularly engaging with a life planning workbook can increase self-awareness by encouraging introspection, self-reflection, and self-discovery. As digital nomads gain a deeper understanding of their thoughts, emotions, and desires, they can make more informed choices that contribute to personal fulfillment.

- Accountability: A life planning workbook can provide a structured framework for tracking progress toward goals and maintaining accountability. By regularly reviewing and updating their plans, digital nomads can stay focused and committed to their objectives, even in the face of challenges or distractions.

- Motivation: Engaging with a life planning workbook can help digital nomads maintain motivation by reconnecting them with their purpose, values, and goals. By regularly reflecting on their aspirations and celebrating their accomplishments, digital nomads can stay inspired and energized throughout their journey.

- Balance: A life planning workbook can help digital nomads ensure they are maintaining balance across various aspects of their lives, such as work, relationships, personal growth, and self-care. By regularly assessing and adjusting their priorities, digital nomads can create a more sustainable and fulfilling lifestyle.

- Adaptability: A life planning workbook can help digital nomads develop resilience and adaptability in the face of change and uncertainty. By regularly reviewing their plans and adjusting their goals as needed, digital nomads can cultivate a growth mindset and learn to embrace new challenges and opportunities.

- Personal growth: A life planning workbook can serve as a catalyst for personal growth by encouraging digital nomads to challenge themselves, step outside their comfort zones, and continuously strive for self-improvement.

By using a life planning workbook, digital nomads can clarify their purpose, find direction, and stay motivated while on the move, ultimately contributing to a more fulfilling and successful location-independent lifestyle.

A collection of prompts and exercises to help you identify what is most important to you and what you want to achieve in life while on the road

Prompts for reflecting on your values, priorities, strengths, and weaknesses as a digital nomad

Reflecting on your values, priorities, strengths, and weaknesses can provide valuable insights and help you make more informed decisions as a digital nomad. Here are some prompts to guide you through this reflection process:

Values:
- What are your top five core values, and why are they important to you?
- How do your values align with your current lifestyle as a digital nomad?
- How do your daily actions and decisions reflect your values?

Priorities:
- What are the most important aspects of your life right now (e.g., work, relationships, personal growth, health)?
- How do you allocate your time and energy to these priorities?
- Are there any areas of your life that need more attention or focus?

Strengths:
- What are your top three strengths, and how do they contribute to your success as a digital nomad?
- How do you leverage your strengths in your work and personal life?
- Can you think of a recent situation where your strengths played a crucial role in achieving a goal or overcoming a challenge?

Weaknesses:
- What are your top three weaknesses or areas for improvement?
- How do these weaknesses impact your life as a digital nomad?
- What strategies or resources can you use to address these weaknesses and minimize their impact on your success?

Additional prompts for reflection:
- What aspects of the digital nomad lifestyle do you find most fulfilling or rewarding?
- What challenges or obstacles have you faced as a digital nomad, and how have you overcome them?

- How do you maintain balance and self-care in your life while on the move?
- What personal or professional goals have you set for yourself as a digital nomad, and what steps are you taking to achieve them?
- How do your relationships and support networks contribute to your success and wellbeing as a digital nomad?

By engaging with these prompts and reflecting on your values, priorities, strengths, and weaknesses, you can gain a deeper understanding of yourself as a digital nomad, identify areas for growth, and make more intentional choices that align with your authentic self.

<u>Exercises for setting clear and achievable goals in various areas of your life, such as career, relationships, personal growth, and travel</u>

Setting clear and achievable goals in various areas of your life can help you stay focused and motivated on your journey as a digital nomad. Here are some exercises to guide you through the process of goal setting in different aspects of your life:

SMART Goals: Use the SMART goal-setting framework to create specific, measurable, achievable, relevant, and time-bound goals in each area of your life.

- Career: Set career goals that align with your values and aspirations. Examples: "Launch my freelance graphic design business within six months" or "Earn a promotion to a senior position within the next two years."

- Relationships: Establish relationship goals that foster deep connections and personal growth. Examples: "Schedule weekly video calls with my closest friends" or "Attend at least two networking events per month to meet new people."

- Personal Growth: Identify personal growth goals that contribute to your overall well-being and happiness. Examples: "Complete a meditation course within three months" or "Read one self-improvement book per month."

- Travel: Set travel goals that align with your desired lifestyle and personal interests. Examples: "Visit three new countries within the next year" or "Learn basic conversational skills in the local language before each trip."

Prioritize: Rank your goals in each area based on their importance and urgency. This will help you allocate your time and energy more effectively and avoid becoming overwhelmed.

Break down goals: Divide each goal into smaller, manageable tasks and milestones. This will make your goals feel more achievable and help you track your progress.

- Identify the key steps required to achieve each goal.
- Estimate the time and resources needed for each step.
- Assign deadlines to each milestone to maintain a sense of urgency.

Visualize success: Spend time visualizing yourself achieving your goals in each area of your life. This can help you maintain motivation and foster a positive mindset.

Create an action plan: Develop a detailed action plan for each goal, outlining the tasks, resources, and timelines needed to achieve it.

- Schedule regular check-ins to monitor your progress.
- Adjust your action plan as needed to account for unexpected challenges or opportunities.
- Celebrate milestones and accomplishments to maintain motivation.

Review and adjust: Regularly review your goals and progress, making adjustments as needed to ensure that they continue to align with your values, priorities, and personal growth.

- Reflect on any changes in your circumstances, priorities, or values.
- Revise your goals and action plans accordingly.
- Set new goals as you achieve existing ones to maintain momentum and personal growth.

By following these exercises, you can set clear and achievable goals in various areas of your life, helping you stay focused, motivated, and fulfilled as a digital nomad.

Tips for breaking down big goals into smaller, more manageable steps

Breaking down big goals into smaller, more manageable steps can make them feel less daunting and help you maintain motivation as you work towards achieving them. Here are some tips for breaking down your goals effectively:

- Identify the key components: Analyse your big goal and identify the main components or tasks required to achieve it. This will give you a clearer understanding of the overall process and help you identify the most critical steps.

- Create sub-goals: Divide your big goal into smaller, more specific sub-goals that can be achieved independently. Ensure these sub-goals are realistic and aligned with the SMART criteria (Specific, Measurable, Achievable, Relevant, and Time-bound).

- Sequence tasks: Determine the logical order of your sub-goals and tasks, taking into account any dependencies or prerequisites. Organize them in a step-by-step sequence, starting with the most foundational tasks and working towards the final goal.

- Set deadlines: Assign deadlines to each sub-goal and task, ensuring they are realistic and achievable. This will help you maintain a sense of urgency and keep your progress on track.

- Break tasks into smaller actions: If a sub-goal or task still feels too big or overwhelming, break it down further into smaller actions or steps that can be easily completed in a single session or a short period.

- Track your progress: Use a goal-tracking tool, spreadsheet, or journal to monitor your progress towards each sub-goal and task. Regularly review and update your progress to maintain motivation and adjust your plan as needed.

- Celebrate milestones: Recognize and celebrate your accomplishments as you complete each sub-goal and task. This can help you maintain motivation and reinforce the positive feelings associated with making progress.

- Adjust your plan as needed: Be flexible and adaptable in your approach. If you encounter unexpected obstacles or opportunities, revise your plan accordingly, and reallocate your resources as needed.

- Maintain a balance: Break down your goals across various areas of your life, such as career, relationships, personal growth, and health, to ensure you maintain a balanced and fulfilling lifestyle.

- Seek support: Share your goals and progress with friends, family, or mentors who can provide encouragement, guidance, and accountability. They can help you stay on track and navigate any challenges that may arise.

By breaking down your big goals into smaller, more manageable steps, you can maintain motivation, track your progress more effectively, and ultimately achieve your desired outcomes.

Guidance for creating an action plan and tracking your progress towards your goals

Creating an action plan and tracking your progress towards your goals can help you stay focused, organized, and motivated throughout the process. Here's a step-by-step guide to create an action plan and track your progress effectively:

- Define your goals: Clearly state your goals, ensuring they are SMART (Specific, Measurable, Achievable, Relevant, and Time-bound). Write them down and keep them visible to maintain focus and motivation.

- Break down goals: Divide each goal into smaller, manageable tasks or sub-goals. This will make them feel more achievable and help you understand the overall process better.

- Sequence tasks: Determine the logical order of your tasks, taking into account any dependencies or prerequisites. Arrange them in a step-by-step sequence, starting with the foundational tasks and working towards the final goal.

- Allocate resources: Identify the resources needed for each task, such as time, money, or additional support from others. This will help you plan more effectively and ensure you have the necessary resources in place to achieve your goals.

- Set deadlines: Assign realistic deadlines to each task and sub-goal, ensuring they are achievable and aligned with your overall timeline. Deadlines help maintain a sense of urgency and keep you on track.

- Create an action plan: Develop a detailed action plan that outlines the tasks, resources, and timelines required to achieve each goal. Use a spreadsheet, project management tool, or physical planner to organize and visualize your plan.

- Track your progress: Regularly monitor your progress towards each task and sub-goal, updating your action plan as needed. Use a goal-tracking tool, spreadsheet, or journal to record your progress and maintain accountability.

- Stay adaptable: Be flexible and open to adjusting your plan as needed. If you encounter unexpected obstacles or opportunities, revise your action plan, and reallocate your resources accordingly.

- Review your goals: Periodically review your goals and progress to ensure they continue to align with your values, priorities, and personal growth. Adjust your goals and action plans as needed to reflect any changes in your circumstances or priorities.

- Celebrate achievements: Recognize and celebrate your accomplishments as you complete each task and sub-goal. This can help maintain motivation and reinforce the positive feelings associated with making progress.

By creating an action plan and consistently tracking your progress, you can stay focused, organized, and motivated throughout your journey towards achieving your goals. Remember to be flexible and adaptable, adjusting your plan as needed to account for unexpected challenges or opportunities.

A section dedicated to self-reflection and introspection, to help you gain deeper insight into your thoughts, feelings, and motivations as a digital nomad.

Self-reflection and introspection are essential for personal growth and understanding, especially as a digital nomad. This section aims to provide guidance and exercises to help you delve deeper into your thoughts, feelings, and motivations, allowing you to make better decisions, adapt to change, and ultimately, find greater fulfillment in your nomadic lifestyle.

The Power of Self-Reflection:
- Understand the benefits of self-reflection and introspection, including increased self-awareness, emotional intelligence, and personal growth.
- Recognize the importance of regularly engaging in self-reflection as a digital nomad, despite the busy and ever-changing nature of the lifestyle.

Mindfulness Practices for Digital Nomads:
- Learn mindfulness techniques that can help you become more present and aware of your thoughts and feelings.
- Explore practices such as deep breathing, body scans, and mindful meditation.

Journaling for Self-Reflection:
- Discover the benefits of journaling as a powerful self-reflection tool.
- Find inspiration with journaling prompts and exercises designed to help you explore your inner world, identify patterns, and gain insights into your experiences as a digital nomad.

Reflecting on Personal Values and Beliefs:
- Engage in exercises to help you identify and understand your core values, beliefs, and motivations.
- Evaluate how well your current lifestyle aligns with your values and beliefs and identify areas for improvement.

Assessing Your Strengths and Weaknesses:
- Conduct a personal SWOT (Strengths, Weaknesses, Opportunities, and Threats) analysis to gain insight into your capabilities and areas for growth.
- Develop strategies to leverage your strengths and overcome your weaknesses as a digital nomad.

Examining Your Emotional Landscape:

- Explore techniques for identifying and understanding your emotions, including emotional intelligence practices and emotion-focused journaling.
- Learn how to manage and regulate your emotions effectively, especially when faced with challenges or stressors in your nomadic lifestyle.

Reflecting on Relationships and Connections:
- Assess the quality of your relationships, both with those you meet on the road and those back home.
- Identify strategies for deepening connections and maintaining healthy relationships despite the distance and transient nature of the digital nomad lifestyle.

Evaluating Your Goals and Aspirations:
- Reflect on your life goals and aspirations, considering how well they align with your values and current lifestyle.
- Revise or set new goals that better align with your evolving priorities, values, and personal growth.

By dedicating time and energy to self-reflection and introspection, you can gain deeper insight into your thoughts, feelings, and motivations as a digital nomad. This understanding will enable you to make better decisions, adapt to change, and ultimately, find greater fulfillment and happiness in your unique lifestyle.

Tips for setting achievable and realistic goals, and tracking your progress towards your dreams while traveling and working remotely

<u>Advice for setting SMART (Specific, Measurable, Achievable, Relevant, and Time-bound) goals as a digital nomad</u>

Setting SMART goals is an essential strategy for achieving success as a digital nomad. This goal-setting framework helps you create clear, actionable objectives that are more likely to be achieved. Here's some advice on setting SMART goals as a digital nomad:

Specific:
- Clearly define your goal, outlining exactly what you want to achieve. Be as detailed as possible to avoid ambiguity.
- Ask yourself the following questions: What do I want to accomplish? Why is it important? How will I achieve it?

Measurable:
- Establish criteria for measuring your progress towards your goal. This allows you to track your progress and know when you have achieved your objective.
- Determine the key performance indicators (KPIs) or milestones that will help you gauge your progress. For example, if your goal is to grow your freelance business, you might measure success by the number of clients, completed projects, or total revenue generated.

Achievable:
- Set goals that are challenging yet attainable, considering your current resources, skills, and time constraints.

- Break down larger goals into smaller, manageable tasks or sub-goals. This makes them feel more achievable and helps you maintain motivation.

Relevant:
- Ensure your goal aligns with your values, priorities, and long-term objectives. This will help you stay motivated and focused on what truly matters to you.
- Assess the relevance of your goal by asking: Is it worth pursuing? Does it align with my values and priorities? Will it contribute to my overall personal and professional growth?

Time-bound:
- Set a realistic deadline for achieving your goal. This creates a sense of urgency and helps you stay on track.
- Be flexible with your deadlines, adjusting them as needed based on your progress, changing circumstances, or new opportunities.

As a digital nomad, it's crucial to set goals that are adaptable to your changing environment and unique lifestyle. Here are some additional tips for setting SMART goals as a digital nomad:

- Balance your goals across various areas of your life, such as career, relationships, personal growth, and travel.

- Regularly review and update your goals to ensure they continue to align with your evolving priorities, values, and lifestyle.

- Be prepared to adjust your goals as your circumstances change, whether due to new opportunities, unexpected challenges, or shifts in your personal or professional life.

- Share your goals with others who can provide support, encouragement, and accountability.

- Keep a goal-tracking journal or use a goal-setting app to monitor your progress and stay motivated.

By setting SMART goals as a digital nomad, you can create clear, actionable objectives that are more likely to be achieved, ultimately enhancing your nomadic lifestyle, and leading to greater personal and professional fulfillment.

The importance of balancing short-term and long-term goals in your life plan

Balancing short-term and long-term goals in your life plan is essential for achieving personal and professional success. Each type of goal serves a different purpose, and maintaining a balance between them can lead to greater fulfillment, motivation, and progress in various areas of your life. Here's why it's important to balance both types of goals in your life plan:

- Prioritization and focus: Long-term goals provide you with a sense of direction and purpose, helping you understand where you want to be in the future. Short-term goals, on the other hand, help you prioritize immediate tasks and maintain focus on the steps required to achieve your long-term objectives. Balancing both ensures you are working towards your overarching vision while also staying on track with day-to-day tasks.

- Motivation and momentum: Achieving short-term goals can provide a sense of accomplishment and boost your motivation, keeping you engaged in your journey towards your long-term objectives. By setting and achieving smaller, short-term goals, you maintain momentum and build the confidence and skills needed to tackle more significant challenges.

- Adaptability and flexibility: Balancing short-term and long-term goals allows you to be more adaptable and flexible in the face of change. Short-term goals can be adjusted more easily as your circumstances or priorities shift, while long-term goals can provide stability and focus in times of uncertainty.

- Personal and professional growth: Balancing both types of goals ensures you are continually growing and developing in various areas of your life. Long-term goals help you think about your overall personal and professional growth, while short-term goals can focus on specific skills or areas of improvement.

- Managing expectations: Long-term goals can sometimes feel overwhelming or unattainable, leading to frustration or a loss of motivation. Balancing these with short-term goals helps manage expectations and break down larger objectives into more manageable tasks, making progress feel more achievable.

- Mitigating burnout: Overemphasis on long-term goals can sometimes lead to burnout or feelings of constant pressure to perform. By incorporating short-term goals and celebrating small wins, you can maintain a healthy balance and reduce the risk of burnout.

To maintain a balance between short-term and long-term goals in your life plan, consider the following tips:

- Set a mix of goals in various areas of your life, such as career, relationships, personal growth, and travel.

- Break down long-term goals into smaller, short-term objectives or milestones to make them more achievable and manageable.

- Regularly review and adjust your goals to ensure they continue to align with your evolving priorities, values, and circumstances.

- Celebrate and reward yourself for achieving short-term goals, acknowledging the progress you've made towards your long-term objectives.

- Maintain a goal-tracking journal or use a goal-setting app to monitor your progress and stay motivated.

By balancing short-term and long-term goals in your life plan, you can enjoy the benefits of both types of objectives, ultimately leading to greater fulfillment, motivation, and success in various areas of your life.

Strategies for overcoming obstacles and staying motivated while working towards your goals

Overcoming obstacles and staying motivated are crucial for achieving your goals. Here are some strategies to help you navigate challenges and maintain motivation while working towards your objectives:

- Break down goals into smaller tasks: Divide your goals into smaller, manageable tasks or milestones. This approach makes progress feel more achievable and helps you maintain motivation as you complete each step.

- Set realistic expectations: Be honest with yourself about what you can achieve given your current resources, skills, and time constraints. Setting realistic expectations can help you avoid disappointment and burnout.

- Develop a strong "why": Remind yourself of the underlying reasons behind your goals. Understanding the purpose and value of your objectives can help you stay motivated and focused, even during difficult times.

- Focus on progress, not perfection: Recognize that setbacks and obstacles are a natural part of the journey. Rather than striving for perfection, celebrate the progress you make along the way, and learn from any mistakes or challenges you encounter.

- Create a support network: Share your goals with friends, family, or colleagues who can provide encouragement, advice, and accountability. Surrounding yourself with a supportive network can help you stay motivated and overcome obstacles.

- Prioritize self-care: Take care of your physical, mental, and emotional well-being by prioritizing self-care activities such as exercise, sleep, and relaxation. Maintaining a healthy balance can help you stay focused and motivated as you work towards your goals.

- Stay organized and plan ahead: Use tools such as planners, calendars, or goal-setting apps to track your progress, set deadlines, and manage your time effectively. Planning and organization can help you stay on track and overcome obstacles more efficiently.

- Develop a growth mindset: Embrace challenges as opportunities for growth and learning. Cultivating a growth mindset can help you stay motivated and resilient in the face of obstacles.

- Be adaptable and flexible: Be prepared to adjust your goals or strategies as circumstances change. Flexibility and adaptability can help you navigate challenges and maintain motivation in the face of unexpected setbacks.

- Reward yourself: Celebrate your achievements, both big and small, by rewarding yourself along the way. This can help boost your motivation and reinforce the positive behaviours that contribute to your success.

- Visualize your success: Regularly visualize yourself achieving your goals and imagine the feelings of satisfaction and accomplishment that will accompany your success. Visualization can be a powerful tool for maintaining motivation and overcoming obstacles.

- Learn from setbacks: When you encounter obstacles or setbacks, take the time to reflect on the experience and learn from it. This can help you develop resilience, improve your strategies, and stay motivated as you continue working towards your goals.

By employing these strategies, you can overcome obstacles, stay motivated, and successfully work towards achieving your goals.

Tips for creating a system for tracking your progress and celebrating your successes along the way

Creating a system for tracking your progress and celebrating your successes is crucial for maintaining motivation and momentum as you work towards your goals. Here are some tips for developing an effective tracking system and acknowledging your achievements:

- Choose a tracking method: Select a method that suits your needs and preferences, such as a physical journal, planner, spreadsheet, or digital app. There are numerous goal-tracking apps available that can help you monitor your progress and set reminders for important milestones.

- Break down your goals: Divide your goals into smaller tasks or milestones, making them more manageable and easier to track. This also allows you to see the progress you're making more clearly and provides opportunities for celebration.

- Set deadlines and milestones: Establish specific deadlines for each task or milestone and mark them in your chosen tracking system. This will help you stay accountable and provide a clear timeline for your progress.

- Monitor progress regularly: Schedule regular check-ins with your tracking system, such as weekly or monthly, to evaluate your progress and make any necessary adjustments to your goals or action plan.

- Reflect on challenges and setbacks: When you encounter obstacles or setbacks, use your tracking system to reflect on the experience, identify any lessons learned, and adjust your strategies if necessary.

- Record your achievements: Document your successes, both big and small, in your tracking system. This can help you maintain motivation and remind you of the progress you've made.

- Set up rewards: Plan rewards for achieving specific milestones or completing tasks. These can be small treats, such as a favourite snack or an evening off, or more significant rewards for major accomplishments, like a weekend getaway or a special purchase.

- Share your progress: Consider sharing your progress with a trusted friend, family member, or mentor who can provide encouragement, support, and accountability.

- Visualize your progress: Create visual representations of your progress, such as charts, graphs, or vision boards, to help you stay motivated and see how far you've come.

- Celebrate your successes: Take the time to acknowledge and celebrate your achievements, whether it's a small milestone or a significant accomplishment. Celebrations can be as simple as treating yourself to something you enjoy or sharing your success with friends and family.

By implementing these tips and creating a system for tracking your progress and celebrating your successes, you can maintain motivation, stay accountable, and work more effectively towards achieving your goals.

Guidance for regularly reviewing and adjusting your goals to reflect your evolving priorities, values, and circumstances as a digital nomad.

Regularly reviewing and adjusting your goals as a digital nomad is important to ensure they remain relevant and aligned with your evolving priorities, values, and circumstances. Here are some guidelines to help you review and adapt your goals effectively:

- Schedule regular check-ins: Set aside time to review your goals on a regular basis, such as monthly or quarterly. This will help you assess your progress, identify any necessary adjustments, and maintain a strong sense of direction and purpose.

- Reflect on your progress: During your check-ins, consider your progress towards each goal. Determine which goals you're on track to achieve, which may require additional effort, and which may need to be adjusted or replaced.

- Re-evaluate your priorities: Consider whether your priorities have shifted since you initially set your goals. Are there new experiences, opportunities, or challenges that have emerged and require your attention? Be honest with yourself about what matters most to you now.

- Examine your values: Reflect on your core values and whether your current goals still align with them. As your values evolve, your goals should evolve with them to ensure they continue to provide meaning and satisfaction.

- Assess your circumstances: Evaluate any changes in your personal or professional circumstances that may affect your goals. Factors such as relationships, finances, work opportunities, or travel plans may influence your ability to achieve certain objectives or necessitate new goals.

- Adjust your goals as needed: Based on your reflections and assessments, make any necessary adjustments to your goals. This may involve setting new goals, revising existing ones, or removing goals that no longer align with your priorities and values.

- Be flexible and adaptable: Embrace the dynamic nature of the digital nomad lifestyle and be open to change. Being adaptable and open to adjusting your goals will help you stay resilient and motivated in the face of uncertainty.

- Seek feedback from others: Share your thoughts and reflections with trusted friends, family members, or mentors who can provide valuable insights, encouragement, and support.

- Set new milestones: After adjusting your goals, establish new milestones and deadlines to guide your progress and maintain your focus.

- Update your action plan: Revise your action plan to incorporate any changes to your goals, ensuring you have a clear and achievable path forward.

By regularly reviewing and adjusting your goals as a digital nomad, you can ensure they remain relevant, inspiring, and aligned with your evolving priorities, values, and circumstances. This will help you stay motivated, focused, and engaged as you continue to pursue your objectives and navigate the unique challenges and opportunities of the digital nomad lifestyle.

CHAPTER 4: FINDING CLARITY AND DIRECTION IN LIFE AS A DIGITAL NOMAD

Strategies for reducing distractions and staying focused on your goals while on the go

Techniques for staying motivated and overcoming obstacles on your personal growth journey as a digital nomad

Staying motivated and overcoming obstacles are essential for personal growth, especially as a digital nomad. Here are some techniques to help you maintain motivation and navigate challenges on your journey:

- Set clear and realistic goals: Establish achievable goals that align with your values, priorities, and aspirations. Break down larger goals into smaller tasks or milestones to make progress feel more attainable.

- Develop a strong "why": Remind yourself of the reasons behind your goals and the benefits you will gain from achieving them. This will help you stay focused and motivated, even during challenging times.

- Embrace change and uncertainty: The digital nomad lifestyle often involves constant change and unpredictability. Develop a flexible and adaptable mindset to embrace these uncertainties and view them as opportunities for growth and learning.

- Cultivate a growth mindset: Emphasize personal growth, learning, and self-improvement over perfection. Acknowledge that setbacks and obstacles are a natural part of the journey and provide valuable learning experiences.

- Create a support network: Build connections with other digital nomads, friends, family, or mentors who can offer encouragement, advice, and accountability. A supportive community can be invaluable in helping you overcome challenges and maintain motivation.

- Prioritize self-care: Take care of your physical, mental, and emotional well-being by prioritizing self-care activities such as exercise, sleep, and relaxation. A balanced lifestyle will help you stay focused and motivated.

- Practice gratitude: Cultivate a habit of gratitude by regularly reflecting on the positive aspects of your life and the progress you've made. This can help you maintain a positive mindset and stay motivated during difficult times.

- Visualize your success: Regularly envision yourself achieving your goals and experiencing the feelings of satisfaction and accomplishment that will result. Visualization can be a powerful tool for maintaining motivation and overcoming obstacles.

- Break tasks into manageable steps: When faced with a challenging task or obstacle, break it down into smaller, more manageable steps. This can help you maintain momentum and motivation by focusing on one step at a time.

- Learn from setbacks: View setbacks and obstacles as opportunities for growth and learning. Reflect on the experience, identify any lessons learned, and adjust your strategies accordingly.

- Celebrate your achievements: Acknowledge and celebrate your successes, both big and small, as they occur. This will help reinforce positive behaviours and maintain motivation.

By implementing these techniques, you can stay motivated, overcome obstacles, and continue to grow and thrive as a digital nomad. Embrace the unique challenges and opportunities of this lifestyle to foster personal growth, self-discovery, and a greater sense of fulfillment.

The role of self-reflection and introspection in finding clarity and direction in life while traveling and working remotely

Self-reflection and introspection play a significant role in finding clarity and direction in life, especially when traveling and working remotely as a digital nomad. The unique lifestyle can present challenges and opportunities that require continuous evaluation and adjustment of your goals, values, and priorities. Here's how self-reflection and introspection can help you find clarity and direction:

- Assess personal values and priorities: Regularly reflecting on your core values and priorities will help you make decisions that align with what truly matters to you. This can lead to greater satisfaction, fulfillment, and a sense of purpose in your life.

- Identify strengths and weaknesses: Introspection allows you to recognize your strengths and weaknesses, enabling you to leverage your skills and work on areas that need improvement. This self-awareness can lead to personal growth, increased confidence, and a better understanding of your unique contributions.

- Evaluate goals and aspirations: Reflection helps you assess your current goals, aspirations, and progress. By regularly revisiting your objectives, you can ensure they remain relevant and aligned with your values and priorities, making adjustments as needed.

- Gain self-awareness: Introspection enables you to understand your thoughts, feelings, and motivations more deeply. This self-awareness can lead to greater emotional intelligence, improved decision-making, and better relationships with others.

- Cultivate resilience and adaptability: Reflection helps you identify patterns in your thoughts, feelings, and behaviours, allowing you to develop strategies for overcoming obstacles and embracing change. This resilience and adaptability are essential in the ever-changing landscape of the digital nomad lifestyle.

- Enhance decision-making: Self-reflection and introspection can improve your decision-making by providing clarity on your values, priorities, and goals. This clarity can help you make choices that align with your long-term vision and lead to greater satisfaction and success.

- Foster personal growth: Reflecting on your experiences and emotions can help you learn from setbacks, recognize personal growth, and develop a deeper understanding of yourself. This insight is valuable for fostering continuous personal development and self-improvement.

- Improve work-life balance: Introspection can help you identify areas where your work-life balance may be off and provide insights into how you can make adjustments to achieve a more harmonious lifestyle.

- Develop a sense of purpose: Self-reflection and introspection can help you uncover your passions, strengths, and unique contributions, which can inform your sense of purpose and direction in life.

- Enhance mindfulness: Regular reflection encourages mindfulness by bringing your attention to your thoughts, feelings, and experiences in the present moment. This mindfulness can lead to increased self-awareness, reduced stress, and a greater appreciation of your surroundings and experiences.

By engaging in self-reflection and introspection as a digital nomad, you can find clarity and direction in your life, even amidst the unique challenges and opportunities of traveling and working remotely.

Examples of successful digital nomads who have used self-reflection and introspection to find clarity and direction in their lives

Here are a few examples of successful digital nomads who have utilized self-reflection and introspection to find clarity and direction in their lives:

- Pieter Levels: Pieter Levels is a successful digital nomad, entrepreneur, and the creator of Nomad List, a platform that helps remote workers find the best places to live and work. Through self-reflection and introspection, he recognized the need for a platform that caters to the growing digital nomad community and successfully built a business around that concept. Pieter continuously assesses his values, goals, and priorities to make informed decisions, which has contributed to his success.

- Celinne Da Costa: Celinne is a life design coach, writer, and digital nomad who has used introspection and self-reflection to find her passion for helping others find their purpose and live authentic lives. After leaving her corporate job, she embarked on a journey around the world to discover her true calling. Through this experience, she recognized her gift for storytelling and coaching, which led her to create her own successful business.

- Matt Kepnes (Nomadic Matt): Matt is a well-known travel blogger and author who found his passion for travel and writing through self-reflection and introspection. He left his traditional career path to explore the world and share his experiences, which eventually led to the creation of his popular blog, Nomadic Matt. Through continuous reflection, he has been able to grow his brand, author several books, and maintain a thriving career as a digital nomad.

- Christine Gilbert (Almost Fearless): Christine is a writer, photographer, and digital nomad who used self-reflection and introspection to transition from her corporate career to a life of travel and adventure. By reassessing her values and priorities, she was able to create a fulfilling life that aligned with her passions for travel, writing, and photography. Christine documents her experiences on her blog, Almost Fearless, which has grown into a successful platform that inspires others to pursue their dreams.

- Jacob Laukaitis: Jacob is a digital nomad, entrepreneur, and travel enthusiast who has leveraged self-reflection and introspection to find clarity and direction in his life. After co-founding an online business, he began traveling the world and documenting his experiences on YouTube. By continuously reflecting on his values, goals, and priorities, Jacob has been able to grow his online presence and inspire others to pursue their passions.

These successful digital nomads have used self-reflection and introspection to gain clarity and direction in their lives, ultimately leading to personal and professional growth. By embracing these practices, they've been able to adapt to the challenges and opportunities of the digital nomad lifestyle while staying true to their values and passions.

Tips for incorporating self-reflection and introspection into your daily routine as a digital nomad

Incorporating self-reflection and introspection into your daily routine as a digital nomad can provide valuable insights and promote personal growth. Here are some tips to help you integrate these practices into your lifestyle:

- Set aside dedicated time: Carve out a specific time each day for self-reflection and introspection. This could be in the morning, evening, or whenever works best for your schedule. Committing to a consistent time will help create a routine and make it more likely that you'll stick to the practice.

- Journaling: Keep a journal to record your thoughts, feelings, and experiences. Writing can be a powerful tool for self-reflection and introspection, helping you process your emotions and gain insights into your mindset and behaviour.

- Practice mindfulness: Mindfulness exercises, such as meditation or deep breathing, can help you become more aware of your thoughts and feelings in the present moment. Set aside a few minutes each day to practice mindfulness and increase self-awareness.

- Reflect on your experiences: As you go about your day, take time to pause and reflect on your experiences. Consider what you've learned from them, how they've shaped your perspective, and what insights you can gain.

- Ask yourself reflective questions: Develop a list of reflective questions that prompt introspection, such as "What am I grateful for?", "What did I learn today?", or "How can I improve?". Regularly asking yourself these questions can help you maintain a self-reflective mindset.

- Use prompts or guided exercises: Use self-reflection prompts, guided exercises, or self-help books to facilitate introspection and self-discovery. These resources can help you explore your thoughts, emotions, and motivations more deeply.

- Embrace solitude: While socializing and networking are essential aspects of the digital nomad lifestyle, it's also important to embrace solitude. Spending time alone allows you to engage in introspection and self-reflection without external distractions.

- Review your goals: Regularly review your short-term and long-term goals to ensure they align with your values and priorities. Reflect on your progress and consider whether any adjustments are needed.

- Engage in creative expression: Use creative outlets like writing, painting, or photography to explore your thoughts and emotions. Creative expression can be a powerful tool for introspection and self-discovery.

- Be patient and persistent: Self-reflection and introspection are ongoing practices that require patience and persistence. Allow yourself the time and space to grow and develop through these practices.

By incorporating self-reflection and introspection into your daily routine as a digital nomad, you can gain deeper insights into your thoughts, emotions, and motivations, ultimately promoting personal growth and enhancing your lifestyle.

The benefits of finding clarity and direction in life as a digital nomad, including improved decision-making, increased focus and motivation, and greater personal fulfilment.

Finding clarity and direction in life as a digital nomad offers numerous benefits that can enhance your overall well-being and success. Some of these benefits include:

- Improved decision-making: With a clear understanding of your values, priorities, and goals, you can make more informed decisions that align with your desired path in life. This can help you avoid making choices that lead to dissatisfaction, frustration, or regret.

- Increased focus and motivation: Having a sense of direction can help you maintain focus on what truly matters to you. This heightened focus can increase your motivation to pursue your goals and dreams, ultimately leading to greater productivity and success.

- Greater personal fulfillment: When you have a clear sense of purpose and direction, you're more likely to feel fulfilled and satisfied with your life. Pursuing goals and dreams that align with your values can bring a sense of accomplishment and contentment.

- Better time management: With a clear direction in life, you can prioritize your time and energy more effectively, focusing on activities that align with your goals and values. This can lead to better productivity and a more balanced lifestyle.

- Enhanced resilience: Understanding your purpose and having a clear direction can help you develop resilience in the face of challenges and setbacks. With a strong sense of purpose, you're more likely to persevere and adapt to changes as you pursue your goals.

- Strengthened relationships: When you have clarity and direction in your life, it's easier to develop meaningful relationships with others who share your values and aspirations. This can lead to a more robust support network that can help you achieve your goals and navigate the challenges of the digital nomad lifestyle.

- Reduced stress and anxiety: A sense of direction can alleviate feelings of uncertainty, stress, and anxiety that often accompany a lack of clarity. By knowing where you're headed and what you want to achieve, you can approach life with greater confidence and peace of mind.

- Greater self-awareness: Gaining clarity and direction in life often involves self-reflection and introspection, which can lead to increased self-awareness. This enhanced understanding of your thoughts, emotions, and motivations can help you better navigate your life and make more informed choices.

- Long-term success: Having a clear direction and purpose in life can contribute to long-term success, both personally and professionally. By aligning your actions with your goals and values, you can create a life that is both rewarding and fulfilling.

- Personal growth: Pursuing clarity and direction in life can lead to personal growth, as you learn more about yourself, develop new skills, and overcome challenges. This growth can contribute to your overall well-being and sense of satisfaction in life.

By finding clarity and direction as a digital nomad, you can experience numerous benefits that can improve your decision-making, focus, motivation, and overall personal fulfillment, leading to a more satisfying and rewarding lifestyle.

Techniques for staying motivated and overcoming obstacles on your personal growth journey as a digital nomad

Strategies for staying focused on your goals and avoiding distractions while on the move

Staying focused on your goals and avoiding distractions can be challenging while on the move, especially as a digital nomad. Here are some strategies to help you stay on track and maintain productivity:

- Set clear goals: Establish specific, measurable, achievable, relevant, and time-bound (SMART) goals to help you stay focused on what you want to achieve. Break larger goals into smaller, manageable tasks to make them more attainable.

- Prioritize tasks: Prioritize tasks based on their importance and urgency. Focus on high-priority tasks first and allocate your time and energy accordingly.

- Create a daily routine: Establish a routine that includes dedicated time for work, self-care, and leisure. A routine can provide structure and help you maintain focus and productivity, even when you're on the move.

- Utilize productivity tools: Use productivity tools and apps to help you stay organized and on track. Examples include task managers, time trackers, and project management software.

- Limit distractions: Identify potential distractions (such as social media, email, or noisy environments) and take steps to minimize them. Set specific times for checking email or social media and use noise-cancelling headphones or work in quiet spaces when possible.

- Set boundaries: Communicate your work hours and availability to friends, family, and colleagues. Establish boundaries to protect your time and maintain focus on your goals.

- Stay accountable: Share your goals with a trusted friend, family member, or mentor who can hold you accountable and provide support. Alternatively, you can join online communities or mastermind groups for digital nomads to connect with others who share similar goals.

- Practice time management: Use time management techniques, such as the Pomodoro Technique or time blocking, to structure your work sessions and maintain focus.

- Take breaks: Regular breaks can help prevent burnout and improve productivity. Schedule short breaks throughout the day to recharge and stay focused.

- Celebrate achievements: Acknowledge your progress and celebrate your accomplishments, no matter how small. This can help you stay motivated and maintain momentum towards your goals.

- Stay adaptable: Be prepared to adjust your plans and goals as needed, based on your circumstances or the opportunities that arise while on the move. Remaining flexible can help you stay focused on what's truly important.

- Maintain work-life balance: Ensure that you allocate time for leisure, exercise, and socializing to avoid burnout and maintain overall well-being. A balanced lifestyle can contribute to greater focus and productivity.

By implementing these strategies, you can stay focused on your goals and minimize distractions while on the move, ultimately enhancing your productivity and success as a digital nomad.

Tips for staying motivated and pushing through challenges and obstacles on your personal growth journey

Staying motivated and overcoming challenges and obstacles on your personal growth journey can be difficult. Here are some tips to help you stay inspired and push through tough times:

- Set clear goals: Establish specific, measurable, achievable, relevant, and time-bound (SMART) goals to provide direction and motivation. Break larger goals into smaller, manageable tasks to make them more attainable.

- Stay focused on your "why": Revisit the reasons behind your goals and remind yourself of their importance regularly. Connecting with your "why" can help you stay motivated and inspired when facing challenges.

- Surround yourself with positive influences: Build a support network of friends, family, and mentors who believe in your goals and can offer encouragement, guidance, and support. Connect with like-minded individuals through online communities, social media, or local meetups.

- Embrace setbacks as learning opportunities: Recognize that setbacks and obstacles are part of the growth process. Learn from your mistakes and use them as opportunities to grow and improve.

- Stay adaptable: Be prepared to adjust your plans and goals as needed, based on your circumstances or new information. Remaining flexible and open to change can help you stay motivated and focused on your personal growth journey.

- Celebrate achievements: Acknowledge your progress and celebrate your accomplishments, no matter how small. This can help you stay motivated and maintain momentum towards your goals.

- Prioritize self-care: Take care of your physical, emotional, and mental well-being. Regular exercise, adequate sleep, and a balanced diet can help you maintain energy and focus. Practice stress-reduction techniques, such as meditation or mindfulness, to stay centred.

- Stay curious and open to learning: Continuously seek out new information, skills, and experiences to expand your knowledge and abilities. Embrace a growth mindset and remain open to learning from others.

- Break tasks into smaller steps: Breaking tasks into smaller, more manageable steps can make your goals feel less overwhelming and more achievable. This can help you maintain motivation and make consistent progress.

- Track your progress: Regularly review your progress towards your goals and make adjustments as needed. Tracking your progress can help you stay motivated and identify areas for improvement.

- Visualize success: Regularly visualize yourself achieving your goals and experiencing the positive emotions associated with success. Visualization can help you stay motivated and focused on your personal growth journey.

- Stay inspired: Find sources of inspiration, such as books, podcasts, blogs, or TED talks, that resonate with your goals and personal growth journey. Engage with these resources regularly to stay motivated and inspired.

By implementing these tips, you can stay motivated and push through challenges and obstacles on your personal growth journey, ultimately enhancing your resilience and success.

The role of positive thinking and visualization in staying motivated and achieving your goals as a digital nomad

Positive thinking and visualization play an important role in staying motivated and achieving your goals as a digital nomad. These techniques can impact your mindset, behaviour, and overall well-being, making them valuable tools for personal and professional growth.

- Improved mindset: Positive thinking helps shift your focus from potential obstacles to possibilities and opportunities. This optimistic mindset can make you more resilient in the face of challenges and more open to exploring new paths towards your goals.

- Increased motivation: Visualizing your goals and the benefits of achieving them can create a strong emotional connection, fuelling your motivation and driving you to work harder. Positive thinking can also contribute to increased motivation by reinforcing your belief in your abilities and chances of success.

- Enhanced self-confidence: Positive thinking and visualization can help you build self-confidence by reinforcing your belief in your capabilities. As a digital nomad, confidence in your skills and abilities can be crucial in navigating unfamiliar situations and seizing opportunities.

- Reduced stress and anxiety: Focusing on positive thoughts and visualizing successful outcomes can help reduce stress and anxiety related to your goals. This can improve your emotional well-being, which in turn can enhance your productivity and overall quality of life as a digital nomad.

- Better decision-making: A positive mindset can lead to better decision-making, as you are more likely to consider a broader range of options and possibilities. Visualization can help you mentally rehearse different scenarios and outcomes, which can aid in making more informed decisions.

- Improved problem-solving: Positive thinking enables you to approach challenges with a solution-oriented mindset, making it easier to identify and implement effective strategies for overcoming obstacles.

- Attraction of opportunities: A positive attitude can make you more approachable and attractive to others, opening doors to new opportunities and connections. Visualization can also help you become more attuned to potential opportunities, as you are mentally prepared for the success you envision.

- Enhanced perseverance: Positive thinking and visualization can help you remain focused on your goals, even when faced with setbacks. By maintaining a positive outlook and visualizing success, you can foster the resilience needed to persevere through challenging times.

To make the most of positive thinking and visualization as a digital nomad, practice these techniques regularly. Set aside time for daily visualization exercises, focusing on your goals and the emotions associated with achieving them. Cultivate positive thinking habits by reframing negative thoughts, expressing gratitude, and surrounding yourself with positive influences. By embracing these practices, you can enhance your motivation, resilience, and success as a digital nomad.

Techniques for building resilience and adapting to change in the digital nomad lifestyle.

Building resilience and adapting to change are essential skills for digital nomads who often face unpredictable situations and challenges. Here are some techniques to help you develop resilience and adaptability in your digital nomad lifestyle:

- Embrace a growth mindset: Cultivate the belief that you can learn and grow from any experience, regardless of its outcome. This mindset helps you view challenges as opportunities for personal development rather than threats or setbacks.

- Practice flexibility: Be open to change and willing to adjust your plans and goals as needed. Embrace new experiences and learn to adapt to different environments, cultures, and work styles.

- Develop a support network: Connect with other digital nomads, friends, and family who can provide emotional support, encouragement, and advice when faced with challenges. Building a strong support network can help you feel more secure and confident in your ability to handle change.

- Prioritize self-care: Taking care of your physical, emotional, and mental well-being is crucial for maintaining resilience. Ensure you get enough sleep, exercise, and eat healthily. Incorporate stress-reduction techniques, such as mindfulness or meditation, into your routine.

- Set realistic expectations: Understand that change and uncertainty are inherent parts of the digital nomad lifestyle. Be prepared for unexpected situations and setbacks, and don't be too hard on yourself when things don't go as planned.

- Focus on what you can control: Accept that there are some aspects of your life that you cannot control or predict. Instead of worrying about these uncertainties, focus your energy on the things you can control, such as your attitude, work ethic, and how you respond to challenges.

- Develop problem-solving skills: Strengthen your ability to solve problems by approaching challenges with a solution-oriented mindset. Break down issues into smaller, manageable steps, and brainstorm potential solutions.

- Learn from past experiences: Reflect on previous challenges and changes you have faced and identify the strategies that helped you successfully navigate them. Use this knowledge to build your resilience and adaptability skills for future situations.

- Cultivate gratitude: Focus on the positive aspects of your life and practice gratitude for the opportunities and experiences that come with the digital nomad lifestyle. This can help you maintain a positive outlook and build resilience in the face of change.

- Celebrate small wins: Acknowledge and celebrate your successes, no matter how small. This can boost your confidence and help you stay motivated to face future challenges.

- Practice patience: Understand that adapting to change and building resilience takes time. Be patient with yourself and trust that you will learn and grow from each experience.

By incorporating these techniques into your daily life, you can develop the resilience and adaptability needed to thrive in the ever-changing landscape of the digital nomad lifestyle.

The importance of self-care and maintaining a healthy work-life balance while on the road

Self-care and maintaining a healthy work-life balance are crucial for digital nomads to ensure their physical, mental, and emotional well-being. When traveling and working remotely, it can be easy to blur the lines between work and personal life, leading to burnout and decreased productivity. Here are some reasons why self-care and work-life balance are important for digital nomads:

- Physical health: Constantly being on the move can take a toll on your body. Prioritizing self-care and ensuring you get adequate rest, exercise, and nutrition is vital for maintaining good physical health and preventing illness.

- Mental health: The digital nomad lifestyle can be isolating and stressful at times. Practicing self-care and establishing a work-life balance can help reduce anxiety, depression, and burnout, contributing to better mental health.

- Emotional well-being: Balancing work and personal life allows you to invest time in nurturing relationships and pursuing hobbies, leading to greater emotional well-being and happiness.

- Increased productivity: Taking regular breaks and setting boundaries between work and personal life can help prevent burnout, leading to improved focus and productivity when you are working.

- Greater job satisfaction: When you maintain a healthy work-life balance, you're more likely to enjoy your work and feel a sense of satisfaction and fulfillment in your career.

- Creativity and innovation: Giving yourself time to recharge and engage in leisure activities can boost your creativity and problem-solving skills, enhancing your performance as a digital nomad.

- Strengthened relationships: Prioritizing work-life balance enables you to invest time and energy into building and maintaining meaningful relationships with friends, family, and other digital nomads.

- Personal growth: Self-care and work-life balance provide opportunities for personal growth and self-discovery, allowing you to explore new interests, learn new skills, and gain a deeper understanding of yourself.

- Adaptability and resilience: Taking care of yourself and maintaining a healthy work-life balance can help you build resilience and adaptability, essential qualities for navigating the challenges and uncertainties of the digital nomad lifestyle.

To maintain a healthy work-life balance and prioritize self-care while on the road, consider setting boundaries for work hours, creating a dedicated workspace, engaging in regular physical activity, staying connected with friends and family, and incorporating stress-reduction techniques, such as mindfulness or meditation, into your routine. By investing in your well-being, you will be better equipped to thrive as a digital nomad.

Examples of successful digital nomads who have used these techniques to stay motivated and overcome obstacles on their personal growth journey.

While specific names and details of individual digital nomads may not be provided, here are some examples of successful digital nomads who have used various techniques to stay motivated, overcome obstacles, and achieve personal growth:

- The mindfulness practitioner: A digital nomad who works as a freelance writer and has incorporated daily meditation and mindfulness practices into their routine. By doing so, they have improved their focus and creativity while reducing stress and anxiety. This has helped them overcome the challenges of loneliness and burnout while maintaining their productivity.

- The goal-oriented traveller: A digital nomad who runs their own online marketing agency has used goal-setting techniques to stay motivated and on track while traveling. They set both short-term and long-term goals, regularly review and adjust their goals, and celebrate their achievements. This has helped them manage their time effectively and maintain a healthy work-life balance, even when constantly on the move.

- The fitness enthusiast: A remote software developer who makes regular exercise a priority, no matter where they are. They have adapted their fitness routine to different environments and have used physical activity as a way to manage stress and maintain their mental and physical health. This has enabled them to stay energized, focused, and overcome the challenges of working in various time zones.

- The creative explorer: A digital nomad who works as a graphic designer and uses creative expression, such as painting or journaling, to process their emotions and gain self-awareness. This practice has helped them cope with the challenges of isolation and culture shock, and they have found inspiration for their work in the various places they've travelled.

- The community builder: A digital nomad who works in social media management and has made an effort to connect with other digital nomads and local communities wherever they go. They have built a strong support network and participate in online forums and meetups. This has helped them overcome feelings of loneliness and maintain a sense of belonging, even when far from home.

- The resilient adventurer: A digital nomad who has developed strong problem-solving and adaptability skills, allowing them to navigate the challenges and uncertainties that come with the nomadic lifestyle. They embrace change, view setbacks as learning opportunities, and practice gratitude for the experiences they encounter.

These examples demonstrate how various techniques, such as mindfulness, goal setting, physical activity, creative expression, networking, and adaptability, can help digital nomads overcome obstacles, stay motivated, and achieve personal growth on their journey.

CHAPTER 5: THE POWER OF EMOTIONAL INTELLIGENCE FOR DIGITAL NOMADS

Understanding the concept of emotional intelligence and its impact on personal and professional relationships as a digital nomad

Techniques for improving emotional intelligence, such as empathy, self-regulation, and effective communication skills while working and living abroad.

Improving emotional intelligence is essential for digital nomads to navigate the complexities of remote work and cross-cultural interactions. Here are some techniques for enhancing emotional intelligence skills such as empathy, self-regulation, and effective communication while working and living abroad:

- Active listening: Practice active listening by giving your full attention to the speaker, making eye contact, and not interrupting. Ask open-ended questions and paraphrase what they have said to ensure you understand their message. Active listening helps improve communication skills and fosters empathy.

- Develop self-awareness: Reflect on your emotions, thoughts, and actions, and try to understand the reasons behind them. Regularly practice mindfulness or journaling to increase self-awareness and recognize patterns in your behaviour that may affect your interactions with others.

- Practice empathy: Put yourself in others' shoes and try to understand their feelings, perspectives, and cultural backgrounds. Be open-minded and non-judgmental and avoid making assumptions about people based on stereotypes.

- Manage your emotions: Learn to recognize your emotional triggers and develop strategies for managing them. This can include taking a break, engaging in deep breathing exercises, or practicing meditation. Developing self-regulation skills helps you maintain composure and respond appropriately in difficult situations.

- Improve nonverbal communication: Be aware of your body language, facial expressions, and tone of voice, as these can convey a lot about your emotions and intentions. Practice maintaining open and friendly nonverbal cues, such as maintaining eye contact, nodding in agreement, and smiling.

- Develop assertiveness: Practice expressing your thoughts and feelings openly and honestly, while respecting others' opinions and feelings. Assertiveness helps you build healthy relationships, communicate effectively, and advocate for your needs.

- Seek feedback: Ask for feedback from colleagues, friends, or mentors to identify areas where you can improve your emotional intelligence skills. Be open to constructive criticism and use it as an opportunity for growth.

- Cultivate cultural awareness: Learn about the customs, traditions, and communication styles of the countries and cultures you encounter while working and living abroad. Understanding cultural differences can help you adapt your communication style and avoid misunderstandings.

- Practice gratitude: Cultivate a habit of gratitude by regularly reflecting on the positive aspects of your life and expressing appreciation for the people around you. Gratitude can help you maintain a positive attitude and improve your relationships.

- Continue learning: Read books, attend workshops, or participate in online courses on emotional intelligence, communication, and interpersonal skills. Continuously working on self-improvement will enhance your emotional intelligence and help you navigate the challenges of working and living abroad more effectively.

The benefits of emotional intelligence in personal growth and relationships for digital nomads

Emotional intelligence plays a significant role in personal growth and relationships for digital nomads, providing numerous benefits that enhance their overall experience and quality of life. Some of the key benefits include:

- Improved communication: Emotional intelligence helps digital nomads communicate effectively with diverse individuals from various cultural backgrounds. They become better listeners, understand non-verbal cues, and can adjust their communication style to suit different situations. This results in smoother and more productive interactions with clients, colleagues, and local communities.

- Enhanced adaptability: With heightened emotional intelligence, digital nomads can adapt more easily to new environments, cultures, and work situations. They become more resilient and better equipped to handle the challenges and uncertainties of a nomadic lifestyle.

- Stronger relationships: Emotional intelligence enables digital nomads to build and maintain meaningful relationships, both personally and professionally. They can empathize with others, manage conflicts, and develop a strong support network that helps them combat loneliness and maintain a sense of belonging while on the road.

- Greater self-awareness: Digital nomads with high emotional intelligence have a better understanding of their own emotions, strengths, and weaknesses. This self-awareness helps them make informed decisions, set achievable goals, and pursue personal and professional growth more effectively.

- Increased emotional well-being: Emotional intelligence contributes to improved mental health and emotional well-being. Digital nomads can manage stress, anxiety, and negative emotions more effectively, leading to greater overall satisfaction with their lifestyle and experiences.

- Better decision-making: Digital nomads with high emotional intelligence are better equipped to make sound decisions by considering not only logical factors but also their emotions and intuition. This leads to more balanced and well-rounded decision-making in various aspects of their life.

- Enhanced collaboration: Emotionally intelligent digital nomads can work more effectively in teams, whether in-person or remotely. They can understand and manage group dynamics, resolve conflicts, and contribute positively to a collaborative work environment.

- Greater empathy: Emotional intelligence enables digital nomads to develop greater empathy for people from different backgrounds and cultures. This empathy helps them connect with others more deeply, fostering a sense of understanding and compassion.

- Personal growth: Developing emotional intelligence is an ongoing process that contributes to personal growth. As digital nomads continue to cultivate their emotional intelligence skills, they can grow as individuals, achieve greater self-awareness, and enhance their overall life experience.

- Increased success: Emotional intelligence is a key factor in achieving personal and professional success. Digital nomads with high emotional intelligence are more likely to navigate their nomadic lifestyle effectively, achieve their goals, and find fulfilment in their work and relationships.

Examples of successful digital nomads who have used emotional intelligence to enhance their lives and relationships.

While specific names of successful digital nomads may not be well-known, there are numerous examples of individuals who have utilized emotional intelligence to improve their lives and relationships while working and traveling. Here are some general examples of digital nomads who have leveraged their emotional intelligence to thrive in their nomadic lifestyle (also please have a look at our eBook 6 - Additional Income Streams):

- Freelance writer: A freelance writer who regularly collaborates with diverse clients from different industries and countries uses their emotional intelligence to communicate effectively, understand their clients' needs, and adapt their writing style to meet expectations. This allows them to maintain long-term relationships with clients, leading to repeat business and a steady income stream.

- Remote team manager: A remote team manager who oversees a team of employees from various cultural backgrounds uses emotional intelligence to understand the unique challenges each team member faces and provide tailored support. By fostering a positive and inclusive work environment, the manager helps their team stay engaged, motivated, and productive.

- Online entrepreneur: An online entrepreneur who runs a successful e-commerce business is in constant communication with suppliers, customers, and partners worldwide. They use emotional intelligence to navigate complex negotiations, resolve disputes, and establish strong partnerships that contribute to their business's growth.

- Travel blogger and influencer: A travel blogger and social media influencer who has built a large following by sharing their experiences and adventures in different countries uses emotional intelligence to connect with their audience on a deeper level. By empathizing with their followers and understanding their needs and interests, they create compelling content that resonates with their audience and leads to more opportunities and collaborations.

- Language and culture coach: A language and culture coach who offers online classes and workshops to help expats and digital nomads adapt to new environments leverages emotional intelligence to understand their students' challenges and provide tailored guidance. By empathizing with their students and offering personalized support, they help them achieve their goals and adapt more effectively to their new surroundings.

These examples illustrate how digital nomads from various fields can use emotional intelligence to enhance their lives and relationships, leading to personal and professional success. By developing emotional intelligence skills, digital nomads can navigate the unique challenges of their lifestyle and make the most of their experiences while working and traveling.

<u>The role of emotional intelligence in building and maintaining meaningful relationships while on the road</u>

Emotional intelligence plays a crucial role in building and maintaining meaningful relationships for digital nomads while on the road. The ability to understand, manage, and express one's emotions, as well as empathize with others, is essential for forming strong connections with people from diverse backgrounds and cultures. Here's how emotional intelligence contributes to meaningful relationships for digital nomads:

- Effective communication: Emotional intelligence helps digital nomads become better listeners and communicators. They can pick up on verbal and non-verbal cues, adjust their communication style based on the situation, and express their thoughts and feelings clearly. Effective communication is key to building trust and rapport with others.

- Empathy and understanding: Digital nomads with high emotional intelligence can put themselves in other people's shoes and understand their feelings, thoughts, and perspectives. This empathy allows them to connect with others on a deeper level, fostering stronger relationships.

- Conflict resolution: Emotional intelligence equips digital nomads with the skills to manage conflicts and disagreements effectively. They can approach difficult situations calmly, listen to different viewpoints, and find mutually beneficial solutions. This skill is essential for maintaining harmony in personal and professional relationships.

- Adaptability: Digital nomads with high emotional intelligence are more adaptable to new environments and cultures. They can quickly adjust to different social norms and customs, making it easier for them to connect with people from various backgrounds and form lasting relationships.

- Emotional support: Emotionally intelligent digital nomads can provide emotional support to others, offering a listening ear, encouragement, or advice when needed. This ability to be there for others strengthens the bonds between individuals and creates a sense of belonging.

- Self-awareness: Digital nomads with high emotional intelligence have a better understanding of their own emotions, strengths, and weaknesses. This self-awareness helps them recognize when they need to ask for help or lean on their support network, fostering interdependence and stronger connections.

- Patience and tolerance: Emotional intelligence enables digital nomads to be more patient and tolerant of differences in opinions, values, and cultures. They can appreciate the diversity of human experiences and learn from others, which enriches their relationships and overall life experience.

- Genuine connections: Digital nomads with high emotional intelligence can form genuine connections with others, as they are more open to sharing their feelings and being vulnerable. This authenticity deepens relationships and creates a foundation for lasting connections.

In summary, emotional intelligence plays a critical role in helping digital nomads build and maintain meaningful relationships while on the road. By developing their emotional intelligence skills, digital nomads can enhance their interpersonal connections and create a supportive network that contributes to a fulfilling and successful nomadic lifestyle.

Tips for incorporating emotional intelligence practices into your daily routine as a digital nomad.

Incorporating emotional intelligence practices into your daily routine as a digital nomad can help you build better relationships, enhance communication, and adapt to new environments more effectively. Here are some tips for integrating emotional intelligence practices into your everyday life:

- Practice mindfulness: Mindfulness exercises, such as meditation or deep breathing, can help you become more aware of your emotions and reactions. Set aside time each day to practice mindfulness and reflect on your emotions.

- Keep a journal: Journaling can help you process your thoughts and feelings, enhancing self-awareness. Write down your experiences, emotions, and thoughts regularly to gain insight into your emotional patterns and triggers.

- Active listening: Make a conscious effort to truly listen when others speak, focusing on understanding their perspective and emotions. Practice maintaining eye contact, nodding in agreement, and asking open-ended questions to encourage deeper conversation.

- Seek feedback: Regularly ask for feedback from your friends, colleagues, or supervisors to gain insight into how others perceive you. Use this feedback to improve your communication skills, emotional awareness, and relationship-building abilities.

- Develop empathy: Practice putting yourself in someone else's shoes and imagining their feelings and experiences. This can help you build empathy and connect with people on a deeper level.

- Learn from different cultures: Embrace the opportunity to learn from people of diverse backgrounds and cultures. Be curious and open-minded and use your experiences to enhance your emotional intelligence.

- Manage your emotions: Recognize your emotions and learn to manage them effectively. Develop strategies for coping with stress, anger, or frustration, such as physical exercise, deep breathing, or talking to a friend.

- Practice gratitude: Focus on the positive aspects of your life and express gratitude for them. Cultivating gratitude can improve your emotional well-being and help you maintain a positive outlook.

- Set boundaries: Be aware of your emotional needs and set boundaries to protect your well-being. Communicate your limits to others and respect their boundaries as well.

- Engage in personal growth: Dedicate time to self-improvement by reading books, attending workshops, or seeking professional guidance on emotional intelligence and personal development.

- Nurture your relationships: Make an effort to stay in touch with friends, family, and colleagues, even when you're on the move. Regular communication and emotional support can strengthen relationships and foster a sense of belonging.

By incorporating these emotional intelligence practices into your daily routine, you can enhance your self-awareness, empathy, communication skills, and adaptability, making it easier to navigate the challenges of the digital nomad lifestyle and build meaningful connections on the road.

The importance of emotional intelligence in navigating the complexities of remote work and travel.

Emotional intelligence plays a crucial role in navigating the complexities of remote work and travel for digital nomads. The ability to understand, manage, and express emotions, as well as empathize with others, can significantly impact one's success and well-being while living a nomadic lifestyle. Here are some reasons why emotional intelligence is important for digital nomads:

- Adapting to new environments: Digital nomads frequently travel to new locations with different customs, cultures, and languages. Emotional intelligence helps them adapt quickly by understanding the emotions and perspectives of the people they encounter, allowing them to form connections and integrate into new communities more effectively.

- Managing stress and burnout: Remote work can be challenging, especially when balancing work, travel, and personal life. Emotional intelligence equips digital nomads with the skills to recognize and manage stress effectively, preventing burnout and promoting mental well-being.

- Building meaningful relationships: Digital nomads often face the challenge of forming and maintaining relationships while on the move. Emotional intelligence helps them communicate effectively, empathize with others, and build lasting connections, creating a support network that is essential for their well-being.

- Effective communication and collaboration: Remote work often involves collaborating with team members across time zones and cultural backgrounds. Emotional intelligence enables digital nomads to communicate effectively, manage conflicts, and build trust with colleagues, leading to successful collaboration and productivity.

- Emotional resilience: The digital nomad lifestyle is full of uncertainties and changes. Emotional intelligence helps individuals develop resilience, allowing them to cope with setbacks, adapt to new situations, and maintain a positive outlook.

- Decision-making: Emotional intelligence enhances self-awareness and understanding of one's values, priorities, and goals, leading to better decision-making in various aspects of life, including work, relationships, and travel.

- Balancing work and life: Digital nomads can struggle to maintain a healthy work-life balance while constantly on the move. Emotional intelligence enables them to recognize their emotional needs, set boundaries, and prioritize self-care, ensuring a sustainable and fulfilling lifestyle.

- Personal growth: Emotional intelligence fosters personal growth by helping individuals gain deeper insights into their emotions, strengths, and weaknesses. This self-awareness promotes personal development and contributes to a sense of purpose and fulfilment.

In conclusion, emotional intelligence is vital for digital nomads as it empowers them to navigate the complexities of remote work and travel with greater ease. By developing their emotional intelligence, digital nomads can enhance their adaptability, communication, relationships, and overall well-being, leading to a more successful and fulfilling nomadic lifestyle.

Techniques for improving emotional intelligence, such as empathy, self-regulation, and effective communication skills while working and living abroad

Strategies for improving empathy and understanding the perspectives of others while working and living abroad.

Improving empathy and understanding the perspectives of others is essential for digital nomads, as it helps them adapt to new environments, build strong relationships, and communicate effectively. Here are some strategies for enhancing empathy while working and living abroad:

- Active listening: When talking with others, focus on truly understanding their perspective and feelings. Listen carefully without interrupting or forming judgments. Maintain eye contact, nod in agreement, and ask open-ended questions to encourage deeper conversation.

- Be curious: Approach new cultures, customs, and languages with an open mind and genuine curiosity. Seek to learn and understand the experiences and perspectives of people from different backgrounds.

- Observe non-verbal cues: Pay attention to body language, facial expressions, and tone of voice, as these can provide valuable insights into the emotions and feelings of others.

- Put yourself in their shoes: Practice imagining what it would be like to experience someone else's situation, feelings, and thoughts. This mental exercise can help you develop a deeper understanding of their emotions and perspectives.

- Practice mindfulness: Mindfulness can help you become more attuned to your own emotions and those of others. Regular mindfulness exercises, such as meditation or deep breathing, can improve your emotional awareness and empathy.

- Engage in cultural immersion: Immerse yourself in the local culture by participating in cultural events, trying local cuisine, and learning the local language. This will help you gain a deeper understanding of the perspectives and experiences of people from different backgrounds.

- Seek feedback: Ask for feedback from friends, colleagues, or supervisors on your empathy and understanding of others' perspectives. Use this feedback to improve your communication and relationship-building skills.

- Read and watch diverse stories: Expose yourself to stories from different cultures and perspectives through books, movies, or documentaries. This can help you develop empathy and understanding of people from various backgrounds.

- Engage in volunteer work or community service: Participating in volunteer work or community service can help you connect with locals on a deeper level and develop empathy for their challenges and experiences.

- Reflect on your experiences: Regularly reflect on your interactions and experiences with people from different backgrounds. Consider how you can improve your understanding and empathy in future encounters.

By implementing these strategies, digital nomads can develop empathy and a better understanding of the perspectives of others, leading to improved communication, stronger relationships, and a more fulfilling experience while working and living abroad.

Tips for regulating your own emotions and reactions to challenging situations while on the road.

Regulating your emotions and reactions in challenging situations is essential for digital nomads, as it helps them navigate the uncertainties of life on the road and maintain mental well-being. Here are some tips for managing your emotions effectively:

- Practice self-awareness: Pay attention to your emotions and try to identify their triggers. Recognizing your emotional state and understanding what causes it is the first step toward regulating your emotions.

- Take a step back: When faced with a challenging situation, take a moment to pause and reflect before reacting. This allows you to respond more thoughtfully and appropriately, rather than letting your emotions dictate your actions.

- Use deep breathing exercises: Deep breathing can help you calm down and regain control of your emotions. When you feel overwhelmed, take slow, deep breaths, inhaling through your nose and exhaling through your mouth.

- Practice mindfulness: Mindfulness techniques, such as meditation, can help you become more aware of your emotions and thoughts. Regular mindfulness practice can improve your emotional regulation and overall well-being.

- Reframe your thoughts: Try to change your perspective on a challenging situation by focusing on the positive aspects or looking for opportunities to learn and grow. This can help shift your emotions and reactions to a more constructive place.

- Establish healthy boundaries: Set clear boundaries to protect your emotional well-being. Know when to say no and communicate your needs and limits assertively.

- Engage in physical activity: Exercise is a great way to release tension and manage your emotions. Regular physical activity can help reduce stress and improve your mood.

- Prioritize self-care: Make time for activities that bring you joy and relaxation. Prioritizing self-care can help you maintain emotional balance and resilience in the face of challenges.

- Seek support: Talk to friends, family, or a mental health professional about your emotions and challenges. Sharing your feelings with others can help you process your emotions and gain valuable insights and advice.

- Practice gratitude: Focus on the positive aspects of your life and express gratitude for them. This can help shift your mindset and improve your emotional regulation.

By implementing these tips, digital nomads can learn to regulate their emotions and reactions more effectively, leading to increased resilience, better decision-making, and improved overall well-being while on the road.

Guidance for improving communication skills and building strong, positive relationships while working remotely.

Improving communication skills and building strong, positive relationships are crucial for digital nomads, as they help create a supportive network and enhance collaboration in remote work situations. Here are some guidelines for developing effective communication skills and nurturing relationships while working remotely:

- Be responsive and available: Respond promptly to messages and emails to demonstrate that you are engaged and reliable. Make yourself available for meetings, even if it means adjusting your schedule to accommodate different time zones.

- Choose the right communication tools: Utilize a variety of communication tools, such as video calls, instant messaging, emails, and project management platforms, to ensure that you can communicate effectively with your team members.

- Be clear and concise: Clearly express your thoughts and ideas to avoid misunderstandings. Use simple language and provide context when necessary to ensure that your message is understood.

- Actively listen: When engaging in conversations, listen attentively, and show interest in what the other person is saying. Ask questions and provide feedback to demonstrate your understanding and engagement.

- Practice empathy and emotional intelligence: Be sensitive to the feelings and emotions of your team members. Show understanding and support for their perspectives and be aware of cultural differences that may impact communication.

- Show appreciation and recognition: Acknowledge the hard work and achievements of your team members. Expressing gratitude and offering praise can strengthen relationships and boost morale.

- Schedule regular check-ins: Arrange regular check-ins with your team members to discuss progress, address concerns, and maintain a sense of connection. This can be done through video calls, phone calls, or even emails.

- Cultivate a sense of team culture: Foster a sense of belonging and camaraderie by sharing personal stories, celebrating team achievements, and engaging in virtual team-building activities.

- Be flexible and adaptable: Be open to new ideas and willing to adapt your communication style to meet the needs of your team members. This can help create a more inclusive and collaborative working environment.

- Seek and provide feedback: Regularly ask for feedback from your team members to identify areas for improvement and growth. Offer constructive feedback to help others improve their communication skills and work performance.

By following these guidelines, digital nomads can enhance their communication skills and build strong, positive relationships while working remotely, ultimately leading to more effective collaboration and increased job satisfaction.

The role of emotional intelligence in conflict resolution and managing difficult situations while on the move

Emotional intelligence plays a vital role in conflict resolution and managing difficult situations, especially for digital nomads who often face unique challenges while on the move. Here's how emotional intelligence can help in resolving conflicts and addressing difficult situations:

- Self-awareness: Being aware of your emotions and recognizing their triggers is essential in understanding your role in a conflict. This awareness helps you take responsibility for your actions, manage your emotions, and approach the situation more objectively.

- Self-regulation: Emotional intelligence allows you to regulate your emotions and maintain control during difficult situations. By keeping your emotions in check, you can respond calmly and thoughtfully, which prevents conflicts from escalating and helps in finding a resolution.

- Empathy: Understanding the feelings and perspectives of others is a crucial component of emotional intelligence. By empathizing with those involved in a conflict, you can gain insight into their motivations and needs, which can help you address the underlying issues and find common ground.

- Active listening: Listening attentively to others without interrupting or imposing your own opinions is a key aspect of emotional intelligence. By actively listening, you can better understand the concerns and needs of all parties, helping you identify solutions that satisfy everyone involved.

- Effective communication: Emotional intelligence enables you to communicate your thoughts and feelings clearly and respectfully. Expressing yourself assertively, without being aggressive or passive, can help prevent misunderstandings and facilitate open dialogue.

- Adaptability: Emotional intelligence helps you adapt your communication style and approach to suit the situation and the individuals involved. This flexibility allows you to better address conflicts and challenges, even in unfamiliar environments or with diverse groups of people.

- Problem-solving: Emotional intelligence aids in identifying the root cause of conflicts and finding creative solutions to resolve them. By focusing on the problem rather than the people involved, you can avoid assigning blame and work collaboratively toward a resolution.

- Building and maintaining relationships: Emotional intelligence helps you build and maintain strong, positive relationships, even in the face of conflict. By addressing conflicts constructively and fostering open communication, you can strengthen relationships and create a supportive network while on the move.

By leveraging emotional intelligence in conflict resolution and managing difficult situations, digital nomads can navigate the complexities of their lifestyle with greater ease, foster healthier relationships, and achieve greater personal and professional success.

Examples of emotional intelligence practices that can be incorporated into your daily routine, such as mindfulness and self-reflection.

Incorporating emotional intelligence practices into your daily routine can have a significant impact on your personal and professional life. Here are some examples of emotional intelligence practices that can be easily integrated into your everyday routine:

- Mindfulness meditation: Spend a few minutes each day practicing mindfulness meditation, focusing on your breath, and observing your thoughts and emotions without judgment. This can help improve self-awareness and emotional regulation.

- Journaling: Regularly writing in a journal is a great way to process your emotions, explore your thoughts, and gain insights into your behaviour patterns. Reflect on your emotions, reactions, and relationships to enhance your self-awareness.

- Emotional check-ins: Throughout the day, take a moment to pause and assess how you're feeling. Recognize and label your emotions to build self-awareness and understand how your emotions may be affecting your thoughts and actions.

- Active listening: Make a conscious effort to practice active listening during conversations. Focus on the speaker, avoid interrupting, and ask clarifying questions to demonstrate your engagement and empathy.

- Empathy practice: Put yourself in other people's shoes and try to understand their perspective, feelings, and needs. This can help you build stronger connections and improve your communication skills.

- Gratitude exercises: Cultivate gratitude by reflecting on the things you're thankful for each day. This practice can help you maintain a positive outlook and improve your emotional well-being.

- Emotional regulation techniques: Practice deep breathing, visualization, or progressive muscle relaxation to help manage stress and regulate your emotions during challenging situations.

- Self-compassion: Treat yourself with kindness and understanding, especially when faced with setbacks or failures. Acknowledge your feelings and remind yourself that it's okay to make mistakes and experience negative emotions.

- Setting boundaries: Learn to set healthy boundaries in your personal and professional life to protect your emotional well-being. Communicate your needs and limits assertively and respectfully.

- Seeking feedback: Regularly ask for feedback from friends, family, or colleagues to gain insights into your emotional intelligence and areas for improvement.

By incorporating these emotional intelligence practices into your daily routine, you can enhance your self-awareness, emotional regulation, empathy, and communication skills, ultimately leading to greater personal fulfilment and success in your personal and professional life as a digital nomad.

The benefits of improving emotional intelligence for personal growth and relationship building as a digital nomad.

Improving emotional intelligence can lead to numerous benefits for personal growth and relationship building as a digital nomad. Here are some of the key advantages:

- Enhanced self-awareness: By developing emotional intelligence, you become more aware of your emotions, thoughts, and behaviours. This self-awareness enables you to recognize your strengths and weaknesses, helping you make informed decisions and cultivate personal growth.

- Better self-regulation: Emotional intelligence helps you manage and regulate your emotions effectively. This skill is particularly valuable for digital nomads, who often encounter stressors and challenges while traveling and working remotely.

- Improved decision-making: With a higher emotional intelligence, you can make more rational and balanced decisions by considering both emotional and logical aspects of a situation. This ability is crucial for digital nomads who need to make important decisions related to work, travel, and relationships.

- Enhanced communication: Emotional intelligence equips you with the skills to communicate your thoughts, feelings, and needs more effectively. This can help you build stronger connections, resolve conflicts, and collaborate more efficiently with colleagues and clients.

- Empathy and understanding: Developing emotional intelligence allows you to better understand and empathize with the feelings and perspectives of others. This skill is particularly valuable when dealing with people from diverse cultures and backgrounds, which is common for digital nomads.

- Stronger relationships: Improved emotional intelligence enables you to build and maintain meaningful relationships, even while on the move. By understanding and managing your emotions and empathizing with others, you can create a supportive network that fosters personal and professional growth.

- Greater adaptability: Emotional intelligence allows you to be more resilient and adaptable in the face of change and uncertainty. This is crucial for digital nomads who often need to navigate new environments, cultures, and work situations.

- Increased self-motivation: Emotionally intelligent individuals are better at setting and achieving goals, as well as maintaining motivation in the face of obstacles. This skill is important for digital nomads, who often need to stay focused and motivated while balancing work and travel.

- Enhanced stress management: Emotional intelligence helps you identify and manage stress more effectively, which is particularly beneficial for digital nomads who often face unique stressors related to remote work and travel.

- Greater personal fulfilment: By improving your emotional intelligence, you can achieve a greater sense of self-understanding and personal fulfilment. This can lead to a more satisfying and rewarding digital nomad lifestyle, both professionally and personally.

In summary, enhancing emotional intelligence as a digital nomad can lead to significant improvements in personal growth, relationship building, and overall well-being, allowing you to thrive in your nomadic lifestyle.

The benefits of emotional intelligence in personal growth and relationships for digital nomads

How emotional intelligence can lead to greater self-awareness and personal growth as a digital nomad.

Emotional intelligence plays a significant role in fostering self-awareness and personal growth as a digital nomad. Here's how it can contribute to these aspects:

- Improved self-awareness: Emotional intelligence involves understanding and recognizing your emotions, thoughts, and behaviours. This heightened self-awareness allows digital nomads to recognize their strengths and weaknesses, identify patterns in their behaviour, and better understand their reactions to different situations. With this understanding, they can make more informed decisions, set realistic goals, and cultivate personal growth.

- Effective self-regulation: As a digital nomad, developing emotional intelligence can help you manage and regulate your emotions effectively. This skill is particularly important when dealing with the unique stressors and challenges associated with remote work and travel. By learning to regulate your emotions, you can maintain a healthy mindset, which is crucial for personal growth.

- Enhanced decision-making: Emotional intelligence allows digital nomads to make more balanced and rational decisions by considering both emotional and logical aspects of a situation. This ability is crucial for personal growth, as it enables you to make choices that align with your values and long-term goals.

- Building empathy and understanding: Developing emotional intelligence helps you better understand and empathize with the feelings and perspectives of others. This skill is particularly valuable for digital nomads who interact with people from diverse cultures and backgrounds. Developing empathy and understanding can foster personal growth by broadening your perspective and enabling you to learn from others.

- Stronger relationships: Emotional intelligence equips you with the skills to communicate effectively, build meaningful connections, and resolve conflicts. For digital nomads, who often need to establish and maintain relationships while on the move, these skills are essential for personal and professional growth.

- Greater adaptability: Emotional intelligence allows digital nomads to be more resilient and adaptable in the face of change and uncertainty. By being able to navigate new environments, cultures, and work situations, you can continue to grow and evolve personally and professionally.

- Increased self-motivation: Emotionally intelligent individuals are better at setting and achieving goals and maintaining motivation in the face of obstacles. This skill is particularly important for digital nomads, who need to stay focused and motivated to balance work and travel effectively.

- Enhanced stress management: Emotional intelligence helps digital nomads identify and manage stress more effectively. By learning to cope with stress and maintain emotional balance, you can create an environment conducive to personal growth and development.

- Greater personal fulfilment: By developing emotional intelligence, digital nomads can achieve a greater sense of self-understanding and personal fulfilment. This can lead to a more satisfying and rewarding lifestyle, both professionally and personally, which ultimately fosters personal growth.

In conclusion, emotional intelligence plays a vital role in promoting self-awareness and personal growth for digital nomads by enhancing self-regulation, decision-making, empathy, relationship building, adaptability, self-motivation, stress management, and personal fulfilment.

The impact of emotional intelligence on building and maintaining meaningful relationships while on the road

Emotional intelligence has a profound impact on building and maintaining meaningful relationships while on the road as a digital nomad. Developing emotional intelligence can enhance interpersonal relationships in various ways:

- Improved understanding and empathy: Emotional intelligence enables you to better understand and empathize with the emotions and perspectives of others. As a digital nomad, you will encounter people from diverse backgrounds and cultures. Empathy allows you to connect with others on a deeper level, fostering stronger and more meaningful relationships.

- Effective communication: Emotional intelligence helps you to express your thoughts and feelings clearly and respectfully, while also being open to the perspectives of others. This ability is essential for building and maintaining strong relationships while working and traveling. Clear and open communication helps to prevent misunderstandings and fosters trust and respect between individuals.

- Active listening: Emotionally intelligent individuals are skilled at active listening, which involves fully engaging with the speaker, asking clarifying questions, and providing feedback. Active listening is a critical skill for building strong relationships, as it demonstrates respect and genuine interest in the other person's thoughts and feelings.

- Conflict resolution: Emotional intelligence equips you with the skills to navigate and resolve conflicts effectively. As a digital nomad, you may encounter challenges and disagreements with others, particularly when dealing with people from different cultural backgrounds. By managing your emotions and approaching conflicts with understanding and empathy, you can maintain harmony in your relationships.

- Emotional support: Emotionally intelligent individuals are better equipped to provide emotional support to others, as they can recognize and respond to the emotional needs of their friends, family, and colleagues. Providing emotional support can strengthen bonds and deepen connections while on the road.

- Adaptability: Emotionally intelligent digital nomads can adapt to various social situations and cultural norms. This adaptability allows them to connect with others more easily, no matter where they are in the world.

- Self-awareness: Emotional intelligence fosters self-awareness, which enables you to understand your own emotions, behaviours, and preferences. With greater self-awareness, you can communicate your needs and boundaries more effectively, leading to healthier relationships.

- Emotional regulation: Emotionally intelligent individuals can regulate their emotions and respond to challenging situations in a balanced and controlled manner. This ability is essential for maintaining healthy relationships, as it prevents emotional outbursts or negative reactions from damaging connections.

- Building trust: Emotional intelligence helps you to build trust with others by demonstrating empathy, understanding, and effective communication. Trust is the foundation of strong and lasting relationships, especially when you're on the road and may not have the opportunity for frequent face-to-face interactions.

In summary, emotional intelligence plays a crucial role in building and maintaining meaningful relationships while on the road as a digital nomad. By developing empathy, effective communication skills, active listening, conflict resolution abilities, emotional support, adaptability, self-awareness, emotional regulation, and trust, you can enhance your relationships and create a supportive network wherever you go.

The role of emotional intelligence in navigating and resolving conflicts while working and living abroad

Emotional intelligence plays a critical role in navigating and resolving conflicts while working and living abroad as a digital nomad. The core components of emotional intelligence - self-awareness, self-regulation, empathy, motivation, and social skills - are essential in managing conflicts effectively. Here's how emotional intelligence can help in conflict resolution:

- Self-awareness: Being aware of your own emotions, triggers, and behaviours is the first step in conflict resolution. By recognizing your emotional state, you can respond more thoughtfully and prevent impulsive reactions that may escalate conflicts.

- Self-regulation: Emotional intelligence helps you regulate your emotions and maintain composure in challenging situations. By managing your emotions effectively, you can approach conflicts calmly and rationally, reducing the likelihood of emotional outbursts or irrational behaviour.

- Empathy: Empathy is the ability to understand and share the emotions of others. When dealing with conflicts, emotional intelligence enables you to put yourself in the other person's shoes, consider their perspective, and respond with sensitivity and compassion. This understanding fosters open communication and paves the way for constructive solutions.

- Active listening: Emotionally intelligent individuals are skilled at active listening, which involves fully engaging with the speaker, asking clarifying questions, and providing feedback. Active listening during conflicts helps to ensure that all parties feel heard and respected, fostering an environment where solutions can be reached.

- Effective communication: Emotional intelligence enhances communication skills, enabling you to express your thoughts, feelings, and concerns clearly and respectfully while also being open to the perspectives of others. Effective communication is crucial for resolving conflicts, as it helps to prevent misunderstandings and ensures that all parties are on the same page.

- Assertiveness: Emotional intelligence allows you to assert your needs and boundaries without being aggressive or confrontational. By being assertive, you can communicate your concerns, negotiate, and work towards a mutually beneficial solution.

- Adaptability: As a digital nomad, you will likely encounter people from diverse backgrounds and cultures. Emotional intelligence helps you adapt to various social situations and cultural norms, enabling you to navigate conflicts effectively and respect differences.

- Collaboration and problem-solving: Emotionally intelligent individuals can work collaboratively to find mutually beneficial solutions to conflicts. By focusing on problem-solving rather than placing blame, emotionally intelligent people can create an environment where all parties can contribute and work together to resolve disputes.

- Building rapport and trust: Emotional intelligence helps to build rapport and trust with others, which can be crucial when resolving conflicts. By demonstrating empathy, understanding, and effective communication, you can foster a sense of trust and cooperation, making it easier to work through disagreements.

In conclusion, emotional intelligence is vital in navigating and resolving conflicts while working and living abroad as a digital nomad. Developing emotional intelligence skills such as self-awareness, self-regulation, empathy, active listening, effective communication, assertiveness, adaptability, collaboration, and trust-building can help you manage conflicts effectively, maintain strong relationships, and create a harmonious work and living environment.

The benefits of emotional intelligence for improving communication and collaboration skills while working remotely

Emotional intelligence is essential for improving communication and collaboration skills while working remotely. Here are some benefits of emotional intelligence in a remote work setting:

- Enhances listening skills: Emotionally intelligent individuals are skilled at active listening, which involves giving full attention to the speaker, asking clarifying questions, and providing feedback.

This ensures that all team members feel heard and understood, fostering a more open and effective communication environment.

- Facilitates clear and concise communication: Emotional intelligence helps individuals express their thoughts, feelings, and concerns clearly and respectfully, while also being open to the perspectives of others. Clear communication is crucial for reducing misunderstandings and ensuring that remote teams are on the same page.

- Builds trust and rapport: Emotionally intelligent people can establish trust and rapport with their colleagues by demonstrating empathy, understanding, and effective communication. Trust is essential for remote teams, as it promotes cooperation and collaboration, even when team members are not physically present.

- Encourages collaboration: Emotional intelligence enables individuals to work collaboratively, as they can understand and respect the feelings, needs, and perspectives of others. This fosters a team environment where everyone contributes and works together towards shared goals.

- Increases adaptability: Emotionally intelligent individuals are more adaptable and flexible, making it easier for them to adjust to the ever-changing nature of remote work. They can better handle unexpected challenges and adapt to new situations, which is essential for maintaining productivity and collaboration in remote teams.

- Improves conflict resolution: Emotionally intelligent people can navigate conflicts effectively by managing their emotions, understanding the feelings of others, and working collaboratively to find mutually beneficial solutions. This ability is vital in remote work settings, where misunderstandings and conflicts can arise due to communication barriers and cultural differences.

- Enhances motivation: Emotional intelligence helps individuals stay motivated and engaged in their work, even in remote settings. By understanding their emotions and managing stress, they can maintain focus and enthusiasm, which leads to better collaboration and productivity.

- Supports inclusive work environments: Emotionally intelligent individuals are more likely to create inclusive work environments that respect and value diverse perspectives. This fosters a sense of belonging and encourages collaboration among team members from different backgrounds and cultures.

- Boosts overall team performance: Emotionally intelligent teams are more likely to communicate effectively, resolve conflicts, and collaborate successfully. This results in improved team performance, higher productivity, and increased job satisfaction for remote workers.

In conclusion, emotional intelligence offers numerous benefits for remote workers, particularly in the areas of communication and collaboration. By fostering empathy, understanding, and effective communication, emotionally intelligent individuals can create a harmonious and productive remote work environment.

Examples of how emotional intelligence can enhance personal relationships, such as friendships and romantic partnerships, while on the move

Emotional intelligence plays a crucial role in enhancing personal relationships while on the move, such as friendships and romantic partnerships. Here are some examples of how emotional intelligence can be beneficial:

- Active listening: Emotionally intelligent individuals are skilled at active listening, which involves giving full attention to the speaker, asking clarifying questions, and providing feedback. This helps create a deeper connection and understanding between individuals, which is essential for maintaining strong relationships while traveling.

- Empathy: Emotionally intelligent people can put themselves in the shoes of others, understanding their emotions and perspectives. This empathy helps to strengthen relationships by making others feel valued and respected, even when you are not physically present.

- Effective communication: Emotional intelligence aids in expressing thoughts, feelings, and concerns clearly and respectfully, while also being open to the perspectives of others. This clear communication is essential for maintaining healthy relationships, especially when distance or travel is involved.

- Adaptability: Emotionally intelligent individuals are adaptable and can adjust to new situations and environments. This flexibility helps maintain relationships while on the move, as they can better handle the inevitable changes and challenges that come with traveling and living abroad.

- Conflict resolution: Emotionally intelligent people can navigate conflicts effectively by managing their emotions, understanding the feelings of others, and working collaboratively to find mutually beneficial solutions. This ability is vital for maintaining healthy relationships while traveling, where misunderstandings and conflicts can arise due to cultural differences or stress.

- Emotional support: Emotionally intelligent individuals can provide emotional support to their friends and partners by recognizing their emotions and offering understanding, empathy, and encouragement. This emotional support can be particularly valuable during challenging times, such as adapting to new environments or dealing with travel-related stress.

- Building and maintaining trust: Emotional intelligence enables individuals to establish trust and rapport with others by demonstrating empathy, understanding, and effective communication. Trust is essential for maintaining strong relationships, especially when distance or travel is involved.

- Nurturing personal growth: Emotionally intelligent people can help foster personal growth within their relationships by encouraging open communication, self-reflection, and emotional exploration. This can lead to a deeper understanding of oneself and one's partner, ultimately strengthening the relationship.

- Respecting boundaries: Emotional intelligence allows individuals to recognize and respect the boundaries of others, ensuring that everyone feels comfortable and respected within the relationship. This is particularly important when traveling, as personal space and boundaries may differ across cultures.

In summary, emotional intelligence can greatly enhance personal relationships, such as friendships and romantic partnerships, while on the move. By fostering empathy, understanding, and effective communication, emotionally intelligent individuals can maintain strong connections with others, even as they navigate the complexities and challenges of a nomadic lifestyle.

The importance of emotional intelligence in promoting well-being and reducing stress while living the digital nomad lifestyle.

Emotional intelligence plays a crucial role in promoting well-being and reducing stress while living the digital nomad lifestyle. Digital nomads often face unique challenges, such as adapting to new environments, overcoming loneliness, and managing a healthy work-life balance. Developing and maintaining emotional intelligence can help mitigate these challenges and foster a sense of overall well-being. Here are some reasons why emotional intelligence is essential for digital nomads:

- Self-awareness: Emotional intelligence helps digital nomads become more self-aware, allowing them to recognize and understand their emotions, triggers, and stressors. This self-awareness enables them to make better decisions, such as when to take a break, seek support, or change their environment.

- Stress management: Emotionally intelligent individuals can identify and manage their stress levels more effectively. They can employ various stress-reduction techniques, such as mindfulness, deep breathing, or physical activity, which are essential for maintaining mental and emotional well-being while on the move.

- Emotional regulation: Emotional intelligence allows digital nomads to regulate their emotions better, preventing them from being overwhelmed by negative feelings such as frustration, loneliness, or anxiety. This ability to manage emotions contributes to improved mental health and overall well-being.

- Building and maintaining relationships: Emotional intelligence helps digital nomads develop and maintain meaningful relationships by fostering empathy, effective communication, and conflict resolution skills. These relationships can provide emotional support and help combat feelings of loneliness or isolation often experienced by digital nomads.

- Adaptability: Emotionally intelligent individuals are more adaptable and can better adjust to new situations and environments. This adaptability is crucial for digital nomads, as they frequently face unexpected changes and challenges.

- Work-life balance: Emotional intelligence allows digital nomads to recognize the importance of balancing work and personal life, helping them set boundaries and prioritize self-care. This balance is essential for maintaining overall well-being and preventing burnout.

- Resilience: Emotional intelligence fosters resilience, enabling digital nomads to bounce back from setbacks and adapt to change more effectively. Resilience is vital for dealing with the uncertainties and challenges associated with the digital nomad lifestyle.

- Emotional well-being: Emotional intelligence contributes to overall emotional well-being by promoting self-awareness, empathy, and effective communication. These skills help digital nomads navigate their emotions and maintain a positive outlook on life, despite the challenges they may encounter.

In summary, emotional intelligence is critical for promoting well-being and reducing stress in the digital nomad lifestyle. By cultivating self-awareness, emotional regulation, and adaptability, digital nomads can better manage the unique challenges they face and maintain a sense of overall well-being while living and working on the move.

CHAPTER 6: THE PROCESS IS DIFFERENT FOR EVERY DIGITAL NOMAD

Recognizing that self-discovery and personal growth is a unique journey for each digital nomad

The importance of finding what works best for you in your self-discovery and personal growth journey.

Finding what works best for you in your self-discovery and personal growth journey is crucial for several reasons. Each individual is unique, and what works for one person may not be as effective for another. By identifying and implementing the methods and practices that resonate with you, you can optimize your personal development, enhance your well-being, and experience a greater sense of fulfilment. Here are some reasons why it's essential to find what works best for you:

- Personalization: Everyone has different needs, goals, values, and preferences. Finding what works best for you ensures that you are engaging in activities and practices tailored to your unique circumstances and requirements, increasing their effectiveness and relevance to your life.

- Motivation: When you find practices and techniques that resonate with you, you are more likely to be motivated and committed to maintaining them. This ongoing motivation helps you stay on track and make steady progress toward your personal growth goals.

- Enjoyment: Engaging in activities that you genuinely enjoy and find meaningful makes the self-discovery and personal growth process more pleasurable. This enjoyment encourages you to continue investing time and effort into your development and helps prevent burnout.

- Sustainability: Finding what works best for you increases the likelihood of maintaining and integrating these practices into your daily routine long-term. Consistency is key to achieving lasting growth and change.

- Self-awareness: As you explore different methods and techniques, you gain a deeper understanding of yourself, your strengths, your weaknesses, and your preferences. This self-awareness is invaluable in guiding your personal growth journey and making informed decisions about the areas of your life you want to develop.

- Adaptability: Understanding what works best for you allows you to be more adaptable and flexible in your approach to personal growth. As your needs and circumstances change, you can adjust your strategies and practices to continue making progress effectively.

- Efficiency: By focusing on the techniques and practices that yield the best results for you, you can make more efficient use of your time and energy. This efficiency allows you to achieve your personal growth goals more quickly and with less wasted effort.

To find what works best for you, it's essential to be open to experimentation and self-reflection. Try different techniques, observe their effects, and adjust your approach based on your experiences and insights. Remember that personal growth is a lifelong journey, and what works best for you may change over time. By staying attuned to your needs and preferences, you can optimize your personal growth journey and experience greater satisfaction and fulfilment in your life.

Examples of different approaches and techniques that have worked for other digital nomads.

Different approaches and techniques may work for various digital nomads depending on their individual needs, preferences, and goals. Here are some examples of methods that have proven successful for others:

- Establishing a routine: Creating a daily routine that includes work, self-care, and leisure activities can help digital nomads maintain a sense of balance and structure in their lives. This routine can include exercise, meditation, goal-setting, and regular meals.

- Coworking spaces: Using coworking spaces can provide a productive work environment, opportunities for networking and social interaction, and a sense of community while working remotely.

- Journaling: Writing down thoughts, feelings, and experiences can help digital nomads process their emotions, gain insights, and track their personal growth over time.

- Time management techniques: Utilizing tools like the Pomodoro Technique or time blocking can help digital nomads manage their workload effectively and maintain a healthy work-life balance.

- Networking and social events: Attending local events and meetups can help digital nomads build connections and create a sense of belonging in their temporary homes.

- Online communities: Joining online forums and social media groups dedicated to digital nomads can provide support, advice, and friendship from fellow remote workers who share similar experiences and challenges.

- Mindfulness and meditation: Practicing mindfulness and meditation can help digital nomads reduce stress, improve focus, and cultivate self-awareness.

- Skill development: Investing time in learning new skills, such as language learning, coding, or photography, can enhance personal growth and make digital nomads more marketable and adaptable in their careers.

- Volunteer work: Engaging in volunteer opportunities can provide a sense of purpose, allow digital nomads to connect with local communities, and give back to the places they visit.

- Goal setting and review: Regularly setting and reviewing personal and professional goals can help digital nomads stay motivated, focused, and aligned with their values and priorities.

Remember that what works for one person may not necessarily work for another. It's essential to experiment with different approaches and techniques to find the ones that resonate with you and best support your personal growth journey as a digital nomad.

Tips for experimenting with different self-discovery exercises and techniques to find what works best for you.

Trying out different self-discovery exercises and techniques can help you find what works best for you. Here are some tips to get started:

- Start with an open mind: Be open to trying new techniques and exercises, even if they seem unconventional or unfamiliar. You never know what might resonate with you and lead to personal growth.

- Take small steps: Don't try to incorporate too many new techniques at once. Start with one or two and give them a fair chance before moving on to others. This will help you avoid feeling overwhelmed and allow you to focus on each technique's effectiveness.

- Be consistent: Dedicate time each day or week to practicing self-discovery exercises. Consistency is crucial for seeing results and determining which techniques work best for you.

- Reflect on your experiences: After trying out a new technique or exercise, take some time to reflect on how it made you feel and whether it helped you gain insights or clarity. This will help you evaluate the effectiveness of the technique.

- Customize your approach: Tailor exercises and techniques to your unique needs, preferences, and goals. For example, if you prefer writing over speaking, try journaling instead of talking through your thoughts with someone else.

- Give yourself time: Personal growth and self-discovery take time. Don't be discouraged if you don't see immediate results or if a particular technique doesn't work for you. Keep experimenting and be patient with yourself.

- Seek inspiration: Look for inspiration from others who have successfully used self-discovery techniques, such as books, blogs, podcasts, or personal stories. Learning from others' experiences can provide valuable insights and ideas for your own journey.

- Share your experiences: Discuss your self-discovery journey with friends, family, or online communities. Sharing your experiences and learning from others can help you gain new perspectives and ideas for techniques to try.

- Keep track of your progress: Document your self-discovery journey by keeping a journal, blog, or digital record. This will help you track your progress, reflect on your experiences, and identify patterns or trends in your personal growth.

- Re-evaluate regularly: Periodically reassess the effectiveness of the techniques and exercises you've tried. This will help you determine which ones are most helpful for your personal growth and make any necessary adjustments to your self-discovery routine.

Remember, self-discovery is an ongoing process, and finding what works best for you may take time and experimentation. Stay open to new experiences, be patient with yourself, and enjoy the journey of personal growth.

The benefits of being open-minded and flexible in your approach to self-discovery and personal growth

Being open-minded and flexible in your approach to self-discovery and personal growth offers various benefits that can enhance your overall well-being and success as a digital nomad. Some of these benefits include:

- Increased self-awareness: Being open to exploring different techniques and practices allows you to gain a deeper understanding of your thoughts, emotions, and motivations. This self-awareness can lead to more informed decision-making and improved overall well-being.

- Personal growth: A flexible approach enables you to learn from diverse experiences and perspectives, fostering personal growth and development. It allows you to discover new passions, interests, and strengths that can enrich your life and contribute to your success as a digital nomad.

- Adaptability: Being open-minded and flexible helps you develop adaptability, an essential skill for digital nomads who often face changing environments and circumstances. This adaptability can make it easier to navigate challenges and thrive in various situations.

- Enhanced creativity: Open-mindedness and flexibility can stimulate creativity by encouraging you to think outside the box and consider alternative perspectives. This creative thinking can lead to innovative solutions and unique insights, both professionally and personally.

- Improved relationships: An open-minded and flexible approach to self-discovery and personal growth can help you develop better communication and empathy skills, fostering stronger and more meaningful relationships with others.

- Reduced stress: Being open to change and willing to adapt reduces the stress that can arise from rigid thinking or resistance to new experiences. This can contribute to improved mental health and overall well-being.

- Lifelong learning: A flexible and open-minded approach promotes a mindset of continuous learning and growth, enabling you to continually evolve and adapt throughout your life.

- Greater resilience: Open-mindedness and flexibility can help you build resilience, making it easier to bounce back from setbacks and adversity. This resilience is especially valuable for digital nomads who face unique challenges in their lifestyle.

- Increased satisfaction: By embracing different experiences and being open to change, you can find greater fulfilment and satisfaction in your life, leading to improved overall happiness and well-being.

- Personalized approach: Being open-minded and flexible allows you to tailor your self-discovery and personal growth journey to your unique needs, preferences, and circumstances, ensuring a more meaningful and effective experience.

In conclusion, adopting an open-minded and flexible approach to self-discovery and personal growth can lead to a more fulfilling, successful, and resilient life as a digital nomad.

The importance of being patient and persistent in your self-discovery journey, even when progress is slow, or setbacks occur.

Being patient and persistent in your self-discovery journey is crucial, especially when progress is slow, or setbacks occur. This patience and persistence can lead to numerous benefits and help you achieve long-term personal growth and fulfilment as a digital nomad. Some reasons why patience and persistence are essential include:

- Personal growth takes time: Growth and self-discovery are not overnight processes; they require consistent effort, reflection, and learning. Being patient allows you to give yourself the time and space necessary to evolve, change, and grow at a sustainable pace.

- Setbacks are learning opportunities: Setbacks and challenges are inevitable in any journey, including self-discovery. Embracing these setbacks as learning opportunities can help you build resilience and adaptability, essential traits for digital nomads.

- Persistence leads to progress: Maintaining persistence in the face of slow progress or setbacks is vital for achieving long-term growth. Consistent effort, even during difficult times, eventually leads to positive change and personal development.

- Building habits takes time: Developing new habits, routines, and practices that support your self-discovery journey can take time and repetition. Patience and persistence can help you stay committed to these habits, even when immediate results may not be apparent.

- Emotional well-being: Patience and persistence contribute to emotional well-being by reducing frustration, stress, and feelings of inadequacy that can arise from expecting rapid progress or fearing failure.

- Self-compassion: Being patient and persistent in your self-discovery journey allows you to practice self-compassion, treating yourself with kindness and understanding when progress is slow, or setbacks occur.

- Achieving long-term goals: Patience and persistence can help you stay focused on your long-term goals, even when short-term obstacles arise. This focus on long-term goals can lead to a greater sense of purpose and fulfilment in your life.

- Enhancing motivation: Maintaining persistence during challenging times can help build a sense of achievement and self-efficacy, enhancing your motivation to continue your self-discovery journey.

- Developing a growth mindset: Practicing patience and persistence can help you develop a growth mindset, which fosters a belief in your ability to learn, adapt, and improve over time. This mindset is particularly valuable for digital nomads who face unique challenges and changes in their lifestyle.

- Personal satisfaction: Staying committed to your self-discovery journey and seeing the progress you make over time can lead to a sense of personal satisfaction, accomplishment, and increased overall well-being.

In conclusion, patience and persistence are essential in your self-discovery journey as a digital nomad. These qualities can help you navigate challenges, setbacks, and slow progress while fostering personal growth, resilience, and fulfilment.

Encouragement to embrace the journey and celebrate each step forward, no matter how small.

Embracing the journey and celebrating each step forward, no matter how small, is an essential part of personal growth and self-discovery. As a digital nomad, you will face unique challenges and experiences that contribute to your personal development. By acknowledging and appreciating each step forward, you cultivate a positive mindset and create a sense of accomplishment that can propel you further on your journey.

- Focus on the process, not just the outcome: Emphasizing the process of growth and learning, rather than solely focusing on the end goal, can help you find joy and satisfaction in each small step forward.

- Practice gratitude: Expressing gratitude for even the smallest of achievements can contribute to a positive outlook, reinforcing a growth mindset and fostering resilience.

- Track your progress: Keep a journal or log of your accomplishments, no matter how small they may seem. This record can serve as a reminder of your progress and a source of motivation when you need it.

- Set small, achievable goals: Break down larger goals into smaller, more manageable tasks. Completing these tasks will provide you with a sense of accomplishment and help maintain your momentum.

- Share your successes: Share your progress with friends, family, or your online community. This not only provides an opportunity for celebration but also helps to create a supportive network that encourages your continued growth.

- Be patient and kind to yourself: Recognize that personal growth is an ongoing process, and setbacks are a natural part of that journey. Treat yourself with kindness and patience as you navigate your path.

- Reflect on your growth: Take time to reflect on your journey and recognize the progress you have made. Acknowledge the challenges you have faced and the lessons you have learned along the way.

- Cultivate a growth mindset: Develop the belief that you can learn, adapt, and improve over time. This mindset will enable you to view each small step forward as a meaningful and valuable part of your self-discovery journey.

- Learn from setbacks: Embrace setbacks and challenges as opportunities for learning and growth. This perspective can help you maintain a positive attitude and stay committed to your journey.

- Celebrate your progress: Reward yourself for your achievements, no matter how small they may be. This celebration can take the form of small treats, words of affirmation, or sharing your accomplishments with others.

In conclusion, embracing your journey and celebrating each step forward, no matter how small, can lead to increased motivation, personal growth, and a more fulfilling digital nomad lifestyle. Stay open to learning and growing and remember to appreciate the progress you make along the way.

Understanding that the methods and techniques discussed in the book may work differently for different people in the digital nomad lifestyle

Recognizing that what works for one person may not work for another in their self-discovery and personal growth journey.

It's essential to recognize that what works for one person in their self-discovery and personal growth journey may not work for another. Each individual is unique, with different experiences, preferences, and circumstances that shape their path to self-improvement. This understanding can lead to greater empathy, respect, and support for others and help you find the right approach to your own growth.

Here are some reasons why it's important to acknowledge the differences in personal growth journeys:

- Different backgrounds and experiences: People come from various cultural, social, and personal backgrounds, which can significantly influence their approach to self-discovery and personal growth. These differences may necessitate distinct strategies and techniques that resonate with their unique experiences.

- Varied learning styles: Everyone has different learning styles, which can affect how they absorb information and apply it to their lives. Some people may prefer visual, auditory, or kinesthetic learning methods, while others may respond better to a mix of styles.

- Personal preferences: Individual preferences can play a significant role in determining the most effective self-discovery and personal growth techniques. Some people may find journaling helpful, while others might prefer meditation or creative expression.

- Unique goals and aspirations: Each person has their own set of goals, dreams, and aspirations that guide their personal growth journey. The methods and techniques that work for one person might not align with the specific objectives of another individual.

- Varying levels of support: The availability of a support network can significantly influence one's personal growth journey. Some individuals may have a strong support system that helps them stay motivated, while others might need to rely more on their internal resources.

- Adapting to change: As people grow and evolve, their self-discovery and personal growth journey may also shift. What works for someone at one stage in their life might not be as effective later on, requiring a change in strategies.

- Emotional intelligence and self-awareness: People have different levels of emotional intelligence and self-awareness, which can impact their self-discovery and personal growth journey. Recognizing and understanding these differences can help individuals tailor their approach to suit their specific needs.

By acknowledging and respecting these differences, you can approach your own self-discovery and personal growth journey with an open mind, experiment with various techniques, and find the best methods that resonate with you. It's essential to remain patient and flexible, recognizing that your journey is uniquely yours and may differ from others. Ultimately, this understanding will lead to a more fulfilling and successful personal growth journey as a digital nomad.

The importance of being open to trying new things and experimenting with different approaches

Being open to trying new things and experimenting with different approaches is crucial in the self-discovery and personal growth journey, especially for digital nomads. This openness allows you to explore various techniques and strategies, ultimately leading to greater self-awareness, self-improvement, and overall satisfaction. Here are several reasons why being open to experimentation is essential:

- Uncovering personal strengths and weaknesses: Experimenting with different approaches can reveal your strengths and areas for improvement. By understanding these aspects of yourself, you can better leverage your strengths and work on your weaknesses, leading to more effective personal growth.

- Discovering what works for you: Being open to trying new things enables you to find the methods that resonate with you and align with your unique preferences, learning styles, and goals. This personalized approach can lead to more successful and fulfilling personal growth.

- Enhancing adaptability: As a digital nomad, you face constant changes in your environment, work, and lifestyle. Embracing new approaches and being open to experimentation can improve your adaptability, helping you navigate these changes with greater ease and resilience.

- Overcoming plateaus: It's not uncommon to encounter plateaus or stagnation in personal growth. Trying new approaches can help you break through these plateaus and continue making progress in your self-discovery journey.

- Fostering creativity and innovation: Experimenting with different techniques and strategies can spark creativity and innovation, enabling you to develop unique solutions to challenges and enhancing your personal growth journey.

- Building self-confidence: Trying new things and stepping out of your comfort zone can boost your self-confidence, as you learn to trust yourself and your abilities to adapt and grow.

- Expanding your perspective: Being open to new experiences can broaden your horizons and expose you to new ideas, cultures, and perspectives. This expanded worldview can enrich your personal growth journey and promote greater understanding and empathy.

- Encouraging lifelong learning: An open-minded and experimental approach fosters a lifelong learning mindset. This continuous learning mentality can help you stay engaged, curious, and motivated in your personal growth journey.

To embrace this experimental mindset, remember to stay curious, maintain a non-judgmental attitude, and practice patience and persistence. By doing so, you'll be better equipped to discover the approaches that work best for you, leading to a more fulfilling and successful personal growth journey as a digital nomad.

Tips for adapting the methods and techniques discussed in the book to your unique needs and circumstances as a digital nomad.

Adapting the methods and techniques discussed in the book to your unique needs and circumstances as a digital nomad is crucial for maximizing their effectiveness. Here are some tips to help you do that:

- Assess your needs and goals: Before you start applying any methods or techniques, take the time to evaluate your current situation, needs, and goals. Consider your values, strengths, weaknesses, and areas where you'd like to improve. This will help you identify which methods are most relevant to you.

- Start small and gradually build up: When introducing new techniques, start with small, manageable changes and gradually build up as you become more comfortable and confident. This will help you maintain momentum and prevent overwhelm.

- Customize the techniques: Modify the methods and techniques to better suit your preferences, learning style, and schedule. For example, if you prefer a visual approach, try creating mind maps or vision boards. If you have a busy schedule, consider incorporating shorter, more focused exercises into your daily routine.

- Combine techniques: Feel free to mix and match different techniques to create a personalized self-discovery and personal growth plan. Experiment with various combinations to find what works best for you.

- Be flexible: As a digital nomad, your circumstances can change quickly. Be prepared to adjust your methods and techniques as needed to accommodate your changing environment, schedule, and goals.

- Seek feedback and support: Share your experiences and progress with friends, family, or fellow digital nomads. They can provide valuable feedback, encouragement, and support, as well as suggest new ideas and techniques to try.

- Monitor your progress: Regularly assess your progress and the effectiveness of the techniques you're using. This will help you identify what's working, what isn't, and where adjustments may be necessary.

- Practice patience and perseverance: Remember that personal growth is an ongoing process, and it takes time to see significant changes. Be patient with yourself, and don't be discouraged by setbacks or slow progress.

- Stay open-minded: Be open to trying new techniques and approaches, even if they seem unconventional or challenging. You may discover new methods that work well for you and your unique circumstances.

- Reassess and adjust: Regularly reassess your needs, goals, and circumstances, and adjust your techniques and methods accordingly. This will help ensure that your personal growth journey remains relevant, engaging, and effective.

By adapting the methods and techniques to your unique needs and circumstances, you'll be better equipped to make meaningful progress in your self-discovery and personal growth journey as a digital nomad.

The benefits of being flexible and adapting your approach as you grow and change over time.

Being flexible and adapting your approach to self-discovery and personal growth as you grow and change over time offers numerous benefits, including:

- Staying relevant: As you evolve, so do your needs, goals, and circumstances. By being flexible and adapting your approach, you ensure that your personal growth journey remains relevant and effective, addressing your current needs and aspirations.

- Encouraging growth: Embracing change and adapting your approach fosters personal growth by exposing you to new ideas, experiences, and challenges. This promotes learning, self-awareness, and emotional intelligence.

- Preventing stagnation: A flexible approach prevents you from becoming stuck in routines or patterns that no longer serve you. By regularly reassessing and adjusting your methods, you maintain momentum and continue to make progress in your personal growth journey.

- Building resilience: Flexibility and adaptability help you build resilience by teaching you to cope with change, uncertainty, and setbacks. This skill is particularly important for digital nomads who often face unpredictable situations and environments.

- Enhancing creativity: A flexible mindset encourages you to explore new possibilities and try different techniques, sparking creativity and innovation. This can lead to fresh insights, breakthroughs, and solutions in various aspects of your life.

- Strengthening relationships: Flexibility in your approach to personal growth can positively impact your relationships, as it demonstrates open-mindedness, empathy, and the ability to adapt to different people and situations.

- Increasing satisfaction and fulfillment: As you adapt your approach to align with your evolving needs and goals, you're more likely to experience a greater sense of satisfaction and fulfillment in your personal growth journey.

- Boosting self-confidence: Successfully navigating change and adapting to new circumstances can improve your self-confidence and belief in your ability to overcome challenges and achieve your goals.

- Promoting balance: A flexible approach allows you to find balance between your personal and professional life, helping you prioritize and manage your time and energy more effectively.

- Encouraging lifelong learning: Embracing flexibility and adaptability promotes a mindset of continuous learning, ensuring that you stay curious, engaged, and committed to your personal growth journey throughout your life.

By being flexible and adapting your approach as you grow and change, you'll be better equipped to navigate the complexities of the digital nomad lifestyle and achieve lasting personal growth and fulfillment.

The importance of being patient and persistent in your self-discovery journey, even when progress is slow, or setbacks occur.

Being patient and persistent in your self-discovery journey is essential, as personal growth is often a nonlinear process with inevitable ups and downs. The following points highlight the importance of patience and persistence, even when progress is slow, or setbacks occur:

- Long-term growth: Personal growth is a lifelong journey, and meaningful change often takes time. Being patient and persistent allows you to continue making steady progress towards your goals, even if the pace is slower than you initially anticipated.

- Developing resilience: Facing setbacks and slow progress can help you build resilience and adaptability, as you learn to cope with challenges and navigate difficult situations. This skill is invaluable in both your personal and professional life, especially as a digital nomad.

- Enhancing self-awareness: Patience and persistence in your self-discovery journey provide you with ample opportunities to learn about yourself, your strengths and weaknesses, and your reactions to various situations. This increased self-awareness can help you make better decisions and improve your emotional intelligence.

- Cultivating self-compassion: By being patient with yourself and acknowledging that setbacks and slow progress are natural, you develop self-compassion. This can help reduce stress, improve your mental health, and foster a more positive relationship with yourself.

- Celebrating small wins: Recognizing and celebrating small victories along the way can help you stay motivated and maintain a sense of progress, even when the overall pace is slow. This can also boost your self-confidence and encourage you to continue pursuing your personal growth goals.

- Overcoming obstacles: Being persistent allows you to overcome obstacles and learn from setbacks, helping you develop problem-solving skills and find alternative paths to reach your goals.

- Maintaining momentum: Patience and persistence help you maintain momentum in your self-discovery journey, ensuring that you continue to make progress even during challenging periods.

- Building habits: Developing new habits and routines often requires persistence and patience. Over time, these habits can become second nature and contribute to lasting change and personal growth.

- Learning from setbacks: When setbacks occur, you can use them as learning opportunities to better understand the obstacles you face and develop strategies to overcome them in the future.

- Achieving personal fulfillment: By being patient and persistent in your self-discovery journey, you are more likely to achieve personal fulfillment and a sense of purpose, as you continue to grow and evolve over time.

In conclusion, patience and persistence are key components of a successful self-discovery journey. By embracing these qualities, you can navigate the challenges and setbacks that arise and continue to make progress towards your personal growth goals.

Encouragement to embrace the journey and celebrate each step forward, no matter how small.

Embracing your self-discovery journey and celebrating each step forward, no matter how small, is an essential part of personal growth and development. Remember that every milestone, regardless of its size, contributes to your overall progress and brings you closer to your goals. Here are some words of encouragement to help you embrace the journey:

- Acknowledge your progress: Take time to recognize and appreciate the progress you've made, even if it seems minor. Reflect on how far you've come and the obstacles you've overcome along the way.

- Be kind to yourself: Treat yourself with kindness, patience, and understanding. Remember that personal growth is a lifelong process, and it's okay to experience setbacks or slow progress.

- Stay present: Focus on the present moment, and don't get too caught up in the destination. Enjoy the process and the experiences you gain along the way.

- Maintain a growth mindset: Cultivate a growth mindset by viewing challenges as opportunities for learning and development, rather than obstacles or limitations.

- Surround yourself with positivity: Seek out people who support and encourage you on your journey. Connect with others who share your goals and values and inspire each other to keep moving forward.

- Practice gratitude: Regularly express gratitude for the progress you've made, the lessons you've learned, and the experiences you've had along the way.

- Keep a record: Document your journey through journaling, photography, or any other method that resonates with you. This can serve as a reminder of your progress and accomplishments over time.

- Be flexible: Be open to change and adapt your approach as needed. Embrace the unexpected and use it as an opportunity for growth.

- Take breaks: Give yourself permission to rest and recharge when needed. Taking breaks can help prevent burnout and ensure that you maintain the energy and motivation to continue on your journey.

- Celebrate your successes: Reward yourself for achieving milestones, no matter how small they may seem. Celebrating your accomplishments can boost your self-esteem and motivation, reinforcing the positive steps you're taking on your journey.

In conclusion, remember to embrace your self-discovery journey and celebrate each step forward. By cultivating a positive mindset and focusing on the progress you're making, you can build a strong foundation for continued growth and personal fulfillment.

Embracing the journey of self-discovery and accepting that it may take time and effort to find your true self while on the road

<u>The importance of being patient and persistent in your self-discovery journey, even when progress is slow, or setbacks occur.</u>

Patience and persistence are crucial in your self-discovery journey, especially when progress is slow, or setbacks occur. The path to personal growth is rarely linear, and experiencing challenges is an inevitable part of the process. Here are several reasons why being patient and persistent is essential:

- Personal growth takes time: Just like physical growth, personal development is a gradual process that unfolds over time. It requires consistent effort, self-reflection, and experimentation to learn and grow.

- Setbacks are learning opportunities: Challenges and setbacks are an essential part of the self-discovery process. They offer valuable insights and help you learn more about yourself, your strengths, weaknesses, and areas that need improvement.

- Embrace the journey: The process of self-discovery is a journey, not a destination. Embracing the journey means accepting that there will be ups and downs along the way, and being patient and persistent through the difficult times will ultimately lead to growth.

- Develop resilience: By being patient and persistent, you build resilience, which is the ability to bounce back from setbacks and adapt to change. Resilience is crucial for personal growth and navigating the challenges of life.

- Keep a long-term perspective: Personal growth is a lifelong process, and it's essential to maintain a long-term perspective. Recognize that slow progress is still progress, and setbacks are temporary.

- Maintain motivation: Being patient and persistent helps you stay motivated in the face of challenges. It enables you to maintain your focus on your goals and continue working towards them despite setbacks.

- Cultivate self-compassion: Patience and persistence help you develop self-compassion, which involves treating yourself with kindness and understanding when things don't go as planned. Self-compassion is vital for personal growth and emotional well-being.

- Develop new skills and habits: It takes time, patience, and persistence to develop new skills and habits. By consistently working on your personal growth, you give yourself the opportunity to learn, grow, and evolve.

- Improve self-awareness: Being patient and persistent in your self-discovery journey leads to greater self-awareness. As you learn more about yourself, you become better equipped to make informed decisions and align your actions with your values and goals.

- Enhance overall well-being: Patience and persistence in your self-discovery journey contribute to your overall well-being. As you grow and develop, you'll experience increased self-esteem, improved relationships, and a greater sense of purpose and fulfillment.

In summary, being patient and persistent in your self-discovery journey is essential to navigate the inevitable challenges and setbacks that come along the way. Embracing this mindset allows you to learn from your experiences, develop resilience, and ultimately achieve personal growth and fulfillment.

Recognizing that self-discovery is a lifelong process and that there is no final destination.

Recognizing that self-discovery is a lifelong process and that there is no final destination is an essential aspect of personal growth. This perspective allows you to approach self-discovery with an open mind, curiosity, and flexibility. Here are some reasons why embracing this mindset is important:

- Emphasizes growth over perfection: Understanding that self-discovery is an ongoing process shifts the focus from seeking perfection to embracing growth. This mindset helps you appreciate your progress and encourages you to keep learning and evolving.

- Encourages adaptability: As you grow and change, your goals, values, and priorities may also shift. Recognizing self-discovery as a lifelong process allows you to adapt and adjust your path as needed, ensuring that your personal growth journey remains relevant and meaningful.

- Builds resilience: By acknowledging that self-discovery is a continuous process, you develop resilience and learn to navigate challenges and setbacks more effectively. This mindset helps you bounce back from difficulties and maintain your motivation for personal growth.

- Fosters curiosity: Embracing self-discovery as a lifelong journey encourages curiosity and a willingness to explore new ideas, experiences, and perspectives. This open-minded approach enriches your personal growth and deepens your understanding of yourself and the world around you.

- Promotes self-awareness: When you recognize self-discovery as an ongoing process, you become more self-aware and in tune with your thoughts, emotions, and motivations. This heightened self-awareness enables you to make more informed decisions and align your actions with your values and goals.

- Enhances well-being: Embracing the lifelong nature of self-discovery contributes to your overall well-being. As you continually grow and evolve, you'll experience increased self-esteem, improved relationships, and a greater sense of purpose and fulfillment.

- Cultivates patience and persistence: Understanding that self-discovery is a lifelong process helps you develop patience and persistence. You learn to accept that progress may be slow at times and setbacks may occur, but you remain committed to your personal growth journey.

- Supports continuous learning: Recognizing that self-discovery has no final destination encourages a commitment to lifelong learning. This mindset helps you stay open to new experiences, information, and insights that can facilitate your personal growth.

- Nurtures self-compassion: When you view self-discovery as a lifelong process, you become more compassionate towards yourself, recognizing that growth takes time and setbacks are natural. This self-compassion supports emotional well-being and resilience.

- Creates a sense of fulfillment: Embracing self-discovery as an ongoing journey fosters a sense of fulfillment and purpose. By continually striving for personal growth, you create a meaningful and rewarding life experience.

In summary, recognizing self-discovery as a lifelong process and understanding that there is no final destination allows you to approach your personal growth journey with an open mind, flexibility, and curiosity. This mindset fosters resilience, adaptability, and a commitment to continuous learning and growth.

The benefits of embracing the journey and enjoying the process of personal growth and self-discovery

Embracing the journey and enjoying the process of personal growth and self-discovery comes with a variety of benefits that can positively impact your life. Here are some of the key benefits:

- Reduced stress and anxiety: Focusing on the journey rather than obsessing over a specific outcome can help you manage stress and anxiety more effectively. This approach allows you to appreciate each step you take, regardless of the size, and to recognize that growth often happens through small, incremental changes.

- Increased self-awareness: Enjoying the process of self-discovery encourages you to tune into your thoughts, emotions, and experiences more deeply. This heightened self-awareness enables you to make more informed decisions, align your actions with your values, and develop a better understanding of yourself.

- Greater resilience: Embracing the journey helps you develop the ability to bounce back from setbacks and challenges. By focusing on the process rather than the end goal, you cultivate resilience and learn to navigate difficulties with greater ease.

- Improved adaptability: Enjoying the process of personal growth enables you to be more adaptable and open to change. This flexibility allows you to adjust your path as needed, ensuring that your personal growth journey remains relevant and meaningful.

- Enhanced well-being: Embracing the journey can contribute to improved mental, emotional, and physical well-being. When you enjoy the process of self-discovery, you are more likely to experience increased self-esteem, stronger relationships, and a greater sense of fulfillment.

- Heightened creativity and curiosity: Focusing on the journey encourages you to explore new ideas, experiences, and perspectives. This open-minded approach can foster creativity and curiosity, enriching your personal growth journey and deepening your understanding of the world around you.

- Stronger relationships: Enjoying the process of self-discovery can lead to healthier, more meaningful relationships. As you grow and evolve, you become better equipped to communicate effectively, empathize with others, and create strong connections.

- Increased motivation and persistence: Embracing the journey can help you maintain motivation and persistence, even in the face of obstacles. When you focus on the process rather than a specific outcome, you are more likely to stay committed to your personal growth and continue moving forward.

- Greater sense of purpose: Enjoying the process of self-discovery helps you develop a deeper sense of purpose and direction in life. As you continually grow and evolve, you are better able to identify your passions and align your actions with your values and goals.

- Increased happiness and satisfaction: By embracing the journey and focusing on the process, you can experience greater happiness and satisfaction in life. This approach allows you to celebrate each step forward, no matter how small, and to find joy and fulfillment in your personal growth journey.

In summary, embracing the journey and enjoying the process of personal growth and self-discovery can lead to numerous benefits, including reduced stress, increased self-awareness, improved well-being, and stronger relationships. By focusing on the process rather than the end goal, you can cultivate resilience, adaptability, and a greater sense of purpose and fulfillment in life.

Tips for staying motivated and committed to your self-discovery journey, even when faced with challenges or obstacles.

Staying motivated and committed to your self-discovery journey can be challenging, especially when faced with obstacles or setbacks. Here are some tips to help you maintain your motivation and continue making progress:

- Set realistic goals: Break down your larger goals into smaller, achievable steps. This will help you maintain momentum and celebrate progress along the way.

- Create a routine: Incorporate self-discovery exercises and practices into your daily routine to make them a regular part of your life. This consistency will help you stay committed to your journey.

- Be patient: Remember that personal growth is a lifelong process, and it takes time to see significant changes. Be patient with yourself and recognize that even small steps forward are valuable.

- Stay curious: Approach your self-discovery journey with curiosity and an open mind. Embrace new experiences and be willing to learn from challenges and setbacks.

- Practice self-compassion: Treat yourself with kindness and understanding when you encounter obstacles. Recognize that setbacks are a natural part of the growth process and remind yourself of your progress thus far.

- Find support: Surround yourself with people who understand and support your self-discovery journey. Share your experiences, challenges, and successes with friends, family, or like-minded individuals who can offer encouragement and advice.

- Reflect on your progress: Regularly review your progress and celebrate your achievements. Reflecting on your growth can help you stay motivated and committed to your journey.

- Adjust your approach: If you find that certain methods or techniques aren't working for you, be willing to adapt and try new approaches. Stay open to change and be flexible in your self-discovery journey.

- Stay inspired: Seek out books, podcasts, videos, or workshops that inspire and motivate you. Learn from others who have embarked on similar journeys and gather ideas for your own growth.

- Focus on the journey: Embrace the process of self-discovery and enjoy the journey, rather than fixating on a specific outcome. This mindset will help you stay motivated and committed, even when progress is slow, or setbacks occur.

Remember, the self-discovery journey is unique for each individual, and it's essential to find what works best for you. By staying patient, open-minded, and flexible, you can maintain your motivation and continue making progress, even when faced with challenges or obstacles.

Encouragement to celebrate each step forward, no matter how small, in your self-discovery journey as a digital nomad.

As a digital nomad embarking on a self-discovery journey, it's essential to celebrate each step forward, no matter how small. Acknowledging your progress, even in seemingly minor ways, can boost your confidence, maintain motivation, and help you appreciate the growth you're experiencing. Here are some words of encouragement to keep in mind:

- Every step counts: Remember that each small step contributes to your overall personal growth. Don't underestimate the power of seemingly minor accomplishments, as they can lead to significant breakthroughs over time.

- Progress is progress: No matter how small the step forward may seem, it's still a move in the right direction. Embrace the progress you make and use it as motivation to continue on your journey.

- Be kind to yourself: Treat yourself with kindness and understanding when you're faced with challenges. Recognize that personal growth is an ongoing process, and setbacks are a natural part of the journey.

- Reflect on your growth: Take time to pause and reflect on how far you've come. By acknowledging the progress you've made, you'll be more likely to maintain your motivation and commitment to your self-discovery journey.

- Share your successes: Share your achievements, no matter how small, with your support network. Friends, family, or fellow digital nomads can offer encouragement and help you celebrate your progress.

- Focus on the journey: Embrace the process of self-discovery and enjoy the journey, rather than fixating on a specific outcome. This mindset will help you stay motivated and appreciate each step forward.

- Reward yourself: Give yourself a small reward or treat when you accomplish a goal or reach a milestone. This positive reinforcement can help you stay motivated and enjoy your self-discovery journey.

- Keep a gratitude journal: Regularly jot down the things you're grateful for, including your small successes and the progress you've made. This practice can help you maintain a positive mindset and stay focused on the growth you're experiencing.

Remember, your self-discovery journey is a personal and unique process, and every step forward is worth celebrating. By acknowledging your progress, staying focused on the journey, and surrounding yourself with a supportive community, you'll be better equipped to navigate the challenges and joys of personal growth as a digital nomad.

The importance of being kind and compassionate towards yourself as you navigate the journey of self-discovery and personal growth.

Being kind and compassionate towards yourself is crucial as you navigate the journey of self-discovery and personal growth. This practice is important for several reasons:

- Cultivate self-acceptance: Embracing self-compassion helps you accept yourself as you are, including your strengths and weaknesses. Recognizing that you are a work in progress allows you to appreciate your unique qualities and encourages growth.

- Foster resilience: Being compassionate towards yourself helps you bounce back from setbacks and disappointments more easily. By acknowledging that challenges are a natural part of the journey, you can learn from your experiences and move forward with greater resilience.

- Reduce self-judgment and criticism: When you practice self-compassion, you are less likely to judge yourself harshly or be overly critical. This mindset creates a healthier internal dialogue and fosters a more positive outlook on your personal growth journey.

- Improve mental well-being: Self-compassion has been linked to increased well-being, reduced stress, and improved mental health. By treating yourself with kindness, you can better manage emotions and maintain a sense of balance in your life.

- Encourage growth and learning: When you approach your personal growth journey with self-compassion, you are more likely to take risks, learn from your experiences, and embrace opportunities for growth and self-improvement.

- Nurture self-care: Being compassionate towards yourself encourages you to prioritize self-care and ensure that your physical, emotional, and mental needs are met. This practice helps you maintain a healthy work-life balance, especially while living the digital nomad lifestyle.

- Build stronger relationships: Practicing self-compassion can lead to greater empathy and understanding in your relationships with others. When you are kind to yourself, you are more likely to extend that kindness and compassion to the people around you.

To cultivate self-compassion in your self-discovery journey, try these tips:

- Practice mindfulness: Observe your thoughts and feelings without judgment and be present in the moment.

- Use positive self-talk: Replace negative self-talk with positive affirmations and statements that validate your feelings and experiences.

- Seek support: Surround yourself with a supportive network of friends, family, or fellow digital nomads who can offer encouragement and understanding.

- Reflect on your accomplishments: Take time to acknowledge your achievements, no matter how small, and recognize the progress you've made on your journey.

- Forgive yourself: Accept that everyone makes mistakes and experiences setbacks. Learn from these experiences and forgive yourself for any perceived failures.

Remember, self-discovery and personal growth are ongoing processes. By being kind and compassionate towards yourself, you can create a positive environment for growth and enjoy the journey more fully.

CHAPTER 7: CONCLUSION FOR DIGITAL NOMADS

A recap of the key concepts discussed in the book for digital nomads

The importance of introspection, emotional intelligence, and self-discovery in the digital nomad lifestyle

In this book, we have explored the importance of introspection, emotional intelligence, and self-discovery in the digital nomad lifestyle. Here is a recap of the key concepts discussed:

- Introspection: The practice of looking inward to examine one's thoughts, feelings, and motivations. Introspection is essential for digital nomads as it fosters self-awareness, resilience, and adaptability in the face of change and uncertainty.

- Emotional intelligence: The ability to recognize, understand, and manage one's emotions and those of others. Emotional intelligence is crucial for digital nomads, as it enhances communication, collaboration, and relationship-building, both personally and professionally.

- Self-discovery: The process of exploring one's inner self, values, beliefs, and desires to gain a deeper understanding of who you are and what you want in life. Self-discovery is important for digital nomads as it helps them find balance, meaning, and purpose in their unique lifestyle.

- Mindfulness and meditation: Techniques that promote self-awareness, reduce stress, and improve focus and concentration. These practices can be easily incorporated into the digital nomad lifestyle, even while on the move.

- Creative expression: Activities such as journaling, painting, drawing, or writing that can help digital nomads tap into their emotions and inner thoughts. Creative expression provides stress relief, improved mood, and increased self-awareness.

- Goal setting and life planning: Setting realistic, achievable goals and tracking progress towards dreams while traveling and working remotely is essential for digital nomads. Regularly reviewing and updating life plans helps maintain focus and motivation.

- Self-care and work-life balance: Prioritizing self-care and maintaining a healthy work-life balance is crucial for the well-being of digital nomads. This includes staying physically, mentally, and emotionally healthy.

- Resilience and adaptability: Building resilience and adapting to change are vital skills for digital nomads, allowing them to navigate the uncertainties and challenges inherent in their lifestyle.

- Embracing the journey: Recognizing that self-discovery and personal growth are lifelong processes, and celebrating each step forward, no matter how small. This mindset helps digital nomads stay motivated and committed to their personal growth journey.

By incorporating these key concepts into their daily routines, digital nomads can enhance their lifestyle, achieve personal fulfillment, and foster meaningful connections with others, even while on the move.

The benefits of incorporating self-discovery exercises and life planning into your daily routine as a digital nomad

In this book, we have discussed the benefits of incorporating self-discovery exercises and life planning into the daily routine of digital nomads. Here is a recap of the key concepts:

- Enhanced self-awareness: Self-discovery exercises, such as journaling, introspection, and creative expression, help digital nomads become more self-aware, which is crucial for personal growth and decision-making.

- Clarity and direction: Life planning and goal setting help digital nomads identify their values, priorities, and objectives, providing a sense of direction and purpose in their lives.

- Improved decision-making: With a better understanding of their values, priorities, and goals, digital nomads can make more informed decisions about their personal and professional lives, leading to greater satisfaction and fulfillment.

- Increased motivation and focus: By setting clear, achievable goals and tracking progress, digital nomads can stay motivated and focused on their personal and professional objectives.

- Resilience and adaptability: Regular self-reflection and life planning help digital nomads build resilience and adaptability, which are essential skills for navigating the uncertainties and challenges of their lifestyle.

- Enhanced relationships: Self-discovery exercises and emotional intelligence practices can improve communication and relationship-building skills, leading to more meaningful connections with others.

- Greater work-life balance: Life planning enables digital nomads to prioritize self-care and maintain a healthy work-life balance, contributing to overall well-being.

- Personal growth and fulfillment: Engaging in self-discovery and life planning activities promotes personal growth and leads to a more fulfilling and satisfying lifestyle for digital nomads.

By incorporating self-discovery exercises and life planning into their daily routines, digital nomads can optimize their lifestyle, achieve personal fulfillment, and foster meaningful connections with others, even while on the move.

The role of emotional intelligence in building meaningful relationships and navigating the complexities of remote work and travel

We have discussed the vital role of emotional intelligence in building meaningful relationships and navigating the complexities of remote work and travel for digital nomads. Here is a recap of the key concepts:

- Improved communication skills: Emotional intelligence helps digital nomads develop effective communication skills, allowing them to express themselves clearly, listen actively, and respond appropriately to others.

- Enhanced empathy: Developing emotional intelligence allows digital nomads to better understand and empathize with the feelings and perspectives of others, fostering stronger, more meaningful connections.

- Conflict resolution: Emotional intelligence equips digital nomads with the skills to manage and resolve conflicts effectively, leading to healthier relationships and more productive collaborations.

- Better adaptability: Emotional intelligence enables digital nomads to adjust their emotions and reactions to various situations, making it easier to adapt to new environments and cultures.

- Stronger professional relationships: Emotional intelligence helps digital nomads build positive professional relationships with clients, colleagues, and partners, improving collaboration and increasing the likelihood of success in their remote work endeavours.

- Nurturing personal relationships: Emotional intelligence plays a significant role in forming and maintaining personal relationships, such as friendships and romantic partnerships, while on the move.

- Stress reduction and well-being: Emotional intelligence contributes to better stress management and overall well-being, making it easier for digital nomads to cope with the challenges and uncertainties of their lifestyle.

By developing and practicing emotional intelligence, digital nomads can enhance their interpersonal skills, navigate the complexities of remote work and travel, and build meaningful relationships that enrich their lives and support their personal growth.

The importance of finding what works best for you in your self-discovery journey and embracing the process.

We have emphasized the importance of finding what works best for you in your self-discovery journey and embracing the process as a digital nomad. Here is a recap of the key concepts:

- Individuality: Recognize that each person's self-discovery journey is unique, and what works for one person may not work for another. Be open to trying different approaches and techniques to find what resonates with you.

- Experimentation: Be open to experimenting with different self-discovery exercises, techniques, and practices to identify which ones have the most significant impact on your personal growth and fulfillment.

- Flexibility: Adapt the methods and techniques discussed in the book to your unique needs and circumstances as a digital nomad. Be willing to change your approach as you grow and evolve over time.

- Patience: Understand that self-discovery is a lifelong process with no final destination. Be patient with yourself and your progress, even when it is slow, or setbacks occur.

- Persistence: Stay committed to your self-discovery journey despite challenges and obstacles. Keep pushing forward and remain open to learning from your experiences.

- Celebrate progress: Embrace the journey and celebrate each step forward, no matter how small. Acknowledging your progress can help keep you motivated and committed to your personal growth.

- Self-compassion: Be kind and compassionate towards yourself as you navigate the journey of self-discovery and personal growth. Recognize that growth often involves challenges and setbacks and treat yourself with understanding and patience.

By finding what works best for you and embracing the self-discovery process, digital nomads can achieve personal growth, self-awareness, and a more fulfilling lifestyle while traveling and working remotely.

Encouragement to continue your journey of self-discovery and personal growth, even when faced with challenges or obstacles.

We have provided encouragement for digital nomads to continue their journey of self-discovery and personal growth, even when faced with challenges or obstacles. Here is a recap of the key concepts:

- Resilience: Develop the ability to bounce back from setbacks and challenges. Cultivate a growth mindset, which allows you to learn from your experiences and view obstacles as opportunities for growth.

- Support: Surround yourself with a supportive network of like-minded individuals, friends, or mentors who can offer encouragement, guidance, and motivation during your journey.

- Self-reflection: Regularly engage in self-reflection and introspection to gain deeper insights into your thoughts, feelings, and motivations. This practice can help you better understand your reactions to challenges and obstacles and develop effective strategies for overcoming them.

- Adaptability: Cultivate adaptability and flexibility, essential skills for digital nomads, to help you navigate the ever-changing landscape of remote work and travel, making it easier to cope with challenges or obstacles that may arise.

- Mindfulness and meditation: Incorporate mindfulness and meditation practices into your daily routine to increase self-awareness, reduce stress, and improve your ability to cope with challenges.

- Embrace the journey: Recognize that self-discovery and personal growth are ongoing processes, and the journey itself is just as important as the destination. Embrace each step forward, no matter how small, and celebrate your progress.

- Stay committed: Remain dedicated to your personal growth journey, even when it's challenging or progress is slow. Keep in mind that perseverance and persistence are key to achieving lasting growth and fulfillment.

By incorporating these concepts and staying committed to your self-discovery and personal growth journey, you will be better equipped to face challenges or obstacles that may arise while living the digital nomad lifestyle.

The significance of self-discovery and personal growth for finding fulfillment and meaning in the digital nomad lifestyle

We've discussed the significance of self-discovery and personal growth for finding fulfillment and meaning in the digital nomad lifestyle. Here is a recap of the key concepts:

- Balance: Achieving balance in various aspects of your life, including work, relationships, and personal development, is crucial for long-term fulfillment and happiness as a digital nomad.

- Introspection: Engaging in introspection helps digital nomads gain a deeper understanding of their values, priorities, and desires, allowing them to make more informed decisions and pursue a lifestyle that aligns with their true selves.

- Emotional intelligence: Developing emotional intelligence enables digital nomads to navigate complex emotions, communicate effectively, and build strong relationships while on the move. This helps create a sense of belonging and fosters personal growth.

- Mindfulness and meditation: Practicing mindfulness and meditation helps digital nomads become more present, focused, and self-aware, leading to a greater sense of fulfillment and well-being.

- Creative expression: Engaging in creative activities, such as journaling, painting, or writing, allows digital nomads to tap into their emotions and inner thoughts, fostering personal growth and self-discovery.

- Goal setting and life planning: Setting clear, achievable goals and creating a life plan provides direction, motivation, and a sense of purpose for digital nomads, enabling them to work towards their dreams and aspirations.

- Adaptability and resilience: Cultivating adaptability and resilience helps digital nomads overcome challenges, embrace change, and continue to grow and evolve on their journey.

By prioritizing self-discovery and personal growth, digital nomads can find meaning and fulfillment in their unique lifestyle, ultimately leading to greater satisfaction and success in their personal and professional lives.

Encouragement to continue the journey of self-discovery and personal growth as a digital nomad

The importance of staying committed and persistent in your self-discovery journey, even when faced with challenges or obstacles.

As a digital nomad, it's essential to stay committed and persistent in your self-discovery and personal growth journey, even when faced with challenges or obstacles. Embracing this journey can help you create a more fulfilling and meaningful lifestyle. Here's some encouragement to keep you motivated:

- Remember your 'why': Reconnect with your reasons for choosing the digital nomad lifestyle and remind yourself of the personal growth and self-discovery opportunities it offers. This will help you stay focused and committed to your journey.

- Embrace the journey: Recognize that self-discovery and personal growth are lifelong processes. There will be ups and downs, but every experience offers valuable insights and opportunities for growth. Embrace each step of the journey and learn from the challenges you encounter.

- Cultivate self-compassion: Be kind and gentle with yourself as you navigate the complexities of the digital nomad lifestyle. Recognize that growth and self-discovery take time, and setbacks are a natural part of the process. Treat yourself with the same understanding and compassion that you would offer to a friend in a similar situation.

- Stay curious and open-minded: Approach your journey with curiosity and a willingness to learn from every experience. Be open to new perspectives, ideas, and techniques that may enhance your self-discovery and personal growth.

- Surround yourself with like-minded individuals: Connect with other digital nomads who share your passion for personal growth and self-discovery. These connections can provide invaluable support, encouragement, and inspiration.

- Celebrate your progress: Acknowledge and celebrate each step forward, no matter how small. Recognizing your achievements can boost your motivation and help you maintain momentum on your self-discovery journey.

By staying committed and persistent in your self-discovery and personal growth journey, you can continue to evolve and thrive as a digital nomad, making the most of the unique opportunities and experiences that your lifestyle offers.

The benefits of continuing to grow and evolve as a person while on the road.

Continuing your journey of self-discovery and personal growth as a digital nomad offers numerous benefits, making the effort to grow and evolve well worth it. Here are some of the advantages you can gain from embracing personal growth while on the road:

- Increased adaptability: Personal growth helps you become more adaptable, enabling you to navigate the constantly changing environment of the digital nomad lifestyle with greater ease and resilience.

- Enhanced self-awareness: As you continue to grow and evolve, you'll develop a deeper understanding of yourself, your strengths, weaknesses, and values. This self-awareness will help you make more informed decisions that align with your goals and priorities.

- Stronger relationships: Personal growth contributes to improved communication and emotional intelligence, fostering stronger connections with others. This can lead to more fulfilling friendships, partnerships, and professional relationships.

- Greater fulfillment and happiness: By continually working on yourself and striving for personal growth, you're more likely to experience a sense of fulfillment and happiness. You'll be better equipped to create a life that aligns with your values and passions.

- Improved problem-solving and decision-making: As you develop and grow, you'll enhance your ability to analyse situations, solve problems, and make better decisions, which is essential for navigating the challenges of the digital nomad lifestyle.

- Increased confidence and self-esteem: Personal growth can lead to increased confidence and self-esteem, empowering you to take on new challenges and pursue your dreams with determination and conviction.

- Broader horizons and personal development: Continually growing and evolving as a person helps you to expand your horizons, learn new skills, and embrace new experiences. This will make your digital nomad journey even more enriching and rewarding.

By continuing the journey of self-discovery and personal growth while on the road, you'll be better equipped to face the challenges and embrace the opportunities that the digital nomad lifestyle offers, ultimately leading to a more fulfilling, meaningful, and enjoyable experience.

Tips for maintaining focus and motivation in your self-discovery journey while living the digital nomad lifestyle.

Maintaining focus and motivation in your self-discovery journey while living the digital nomad lifestyle can be challenging, but with the right approach, you can stay on track. Here are some tips to help you maintain focus and motivation:

- Set clear goals: Having specific, measurable, achievable, relevant, and time-bound (SMART) goals will provide direction and help you stay focused on your personal growth journey.

- Break goals into smaller steps: Divide your larger goals into smaller, manageable steps. This will make your journey feel less overwhelming and provide you with a sense of accomplishment as you complete each step.

- Establish a routine: Creating a routine that incorporates self-discovery and personal growth activities will help you stay consistent in your efforts. Schedule time for reflection, journaling, meditation, or other practices that support your journey.

- Stay accountable: Share your goals with someone you trust or join a community of like-minded individuals who can offer support and encouragement. Accountability can help you stay committed and motivated.

- Celebrate small victories: Acknowledge and celebrate your progress, no matter how small. Recognizing your achievements can boost your motivation and help you maintain momentum.

- Stay flexible and adaptable: Be open to changing your approach if something isn't working. Adjust your goals and strategies as needed and be willing to try new methods or techniques that may better suit your needs and circumstances.

- Maintain a growth mindset: Embrace challenges as opportunities for growth and view setbacks as learning experiences. Cultivating a growth mindset can help you stay motivated and focused on your journey.

- Practice self-compassion: Be kind to yourself and remember that personal growth is an ongoing process. Don't be too hard on yourself if you face setbacks or don't see immediate results.

- Find inspiration: Surround yourself with inspiring books, podcasts, and people who share your passion for personal growth. This can help you stay motivated and engaged in your journey.

- Reflect regularly: Periodically assess your progress, celebrate your achievements, and adjust your goals as needed. Reflecting on your journey can help you stay focused on your personal growth and ensure you are moving in the right direction.

By incorporating these tips into your daily life, you can maintain focus and motivation in your self-discovery journey while living the digital nomad lifestyle, ultimately leading to greater personal growth and fulfillment.

The significance of self-discovery and personal growth for finding happiness, fulfillment, and meaning in life

Embarking on a journey of self-discovery and personal growth as a digital nomad holds immense significance in finding happiness, fulfillment, and meaning in life. The process helps you develop a deeper understanding of yourself, your values, and your passions. Here are some reasons why self-discovery and personal growth are vital for your overall well-being:

- Self-awareness: As you explore your thoughts, emotions, and beliefs, you gain a better understanding of who you are and what truly matters to you. This self-awareness allows you to make more informed decisions about your life and work, leading to greater satisfaction and alignment with your true self.

- Emotional well-being: Engaging in personal growth practices such as meditation, journaling, and mindfulness can help you manage stress, reduce anxiety, and improve your overall emotional well-being. Emotional health is a critical aspect of finding happiness and fulfillment in life.

- Stronger relationships: Self-discovery and personal growth can lead to improved emotional intelligence, which enhances your ability to empathize, communicate effectively, and form deeper connections with others. Meaningful relationships are essential for happiness and fulfillment.

- Sense of purpose: As you gain clarity on your values, strengths, and passions, you can align your life and work with your unique purpose. A sense of purpose provides meaning and direction, ultimately contributing to greater happiness and fulfillment.

- Adaptability and resilience: Personal growth practices equip you with the skills and mindset necessary to adapt to change and overcome challenges. Resilience is crucial for navigating the digital nomad lifestyle and maintaining overall well-being.

- Continued growth: Embracing personal growth as a lifelong journey keeps you engaged, motivated, and open to new experiences. This mindset fosters a sense of curiosity, exploration, and learning that enriches your life and prevents stagnation.

- Self-actualization: The process of self-discovery and personal growth supports your journey towards self-actualization, the realization of your fullest potential. Achieving this state can bring profound happiness, fulfillment, and meaning to your life.

By committing to the journey of self-discovery and personal growth as a digital nomad, you can unlock the potential for greater happiness, fulfillment, and meaning in your life. Embrace the process, celebrate your progress, and continue moving forward on your unique path.

A final message of encouragement and support for digital nomads on their journey of self-discovery and personal growth.
Dear Digital Nomad,

As you embark on your journey of self-discovery and personal growth, remember that you are not alone. This path is filled with challenges, triumphs, and countless opportunities for growth and learning. Embrace the unique experiences that come with the digital nomad lifestyle and allow yourself to grow and evolve along the way. Book 6 - Additional Income Streams

Be kind to yourself, recognizing that personal growth is a lifelong process, and setbacks are a natural part of the journey. Celebrate your progress, no matter how small, and cherish each step forward. Stay curious, open-minded, and adaptable, as these qualities will serve you well in both your personal and professional life.

Connect with fellow digital nomads, share your experiences, and learn from each other. Building a supportive community will not only enrich your life but also provide the motivation and encouragement you need during challenging times.

Remember that self-discovery and personal growth are essential to finding happiness, fulfillment, and meaning in your life. By staying committed to this journey, you can unlock your fullest potential and create a life that truly reflects your values, passions, and dreams.

You are capable of achieving great things, and the world has so much to offer. Keep pushing yourself, stay focused on your goals, and embrace the adventure of self-discovery and personal growth as a digital nomad. Your journey is unique, beautiful, and filled with endless possibilities. Embrace it, enjoy it, and above all, believe in yourself.

With warm encouragement and support,

Your fellow traveller, ConnectNomads.com, on the journey of self-discovery and personal growth

We know you appreciate how valuable reviews are to both the creators and the potential buyers of a book. Reviews help authors to improve their writing and encourage them to continue creating content that readers enjoy. They also help other readers to make informed decisions about whether a book is right for them.

So, if you have purchased this book and found it helpful, informative, or enjoyable, we implore you to take a few minutes to leave a review. Your feedback could be the deciding factor for someone else trying to decide whether to buy this book or not.

Your review doesn't need to be lengthy or formal, just an honest account of your experience with the book. Even a few sentences can make a big difference. So please, consider leaving a review and help support the author and potential readers in making an informed decision.

Thank you for your time and support.